ENCOUNTER
THROUGH THE
BIBLE

MATTHEW | MARK

Copyright © Scripture Union 2011
First published 2011
ISBN 978 1 84427 577 9

Scripture Union England and Wales
207–209 Queensway, Bletchley, Milton Keynes MK2 2EB, UK
Email: info@scriptureunion.org.uk
Website: www.scriptureunion.org.uk

Scripture Union Australia
Locked Bag 2, Central Coast Business Centre, NSW 2252
Website: www.su.org.au

Scripture Union USA
PO Box 987, Valley Forge, PA 19482
Website: www.scriptureunion.org

The daily devotional notes for *Encounter through the Bible* have previously appeared in *Encounter with God*, a Scripture Union dated daily Bible guide.

The introductory material is adapted for this series from *The Bible in Outline* (Scripture Union, 1985) and *Explorer's Guide to the Bible* (John Grayston, Scripture Union, 2008)

British Library Cataloguing-in-Publication Data: a catalogue record of this book is available from the British Library.

Printed and bound in India by Nutech Print Services
Cover design by Heather Knight

Scripture Union is an international Christian charity working with churches in more than 130 countries, providing resources to bring the good news about Jesus to children young people and families and to encourage them to develop spiritually through the Bible and prayer. As well as co-ordinating a network of volunteers, staff and associates who run holidays, church-based events and school groups, we produce a wide range of publications and support those who use our resources through training programmes.

CONTENTS

MEETING GOD

For many years Christians throughout the world have found the 'Scripture Union method' a tremendous help in deepening their relationship with God as they read the Bible. Here is a modern version of that method, which aims to help you to make your time with God a true meeting with him. You may like to refer to it each day as a supplement to the comments in this volume.

COME TO GOD as you are. Worship him for his power, greatness and majesty. Bring him your feelings and needs. Ask for his Holy Spirit to help you understand and respond to what you read.

READ the Bible passage slowly and thoughtfully, listening out for what God is saying to you.

TALK WITH GOD about what you have read. These suggestions may help you:

- 'Lord, thank you for your Word to me today. What special message are you shouting out to me, or whispering to me, in these verses?'

- 'Lord, I want to meet you here; tell me more about yourself, Father, Son and Holy Spirit, in these verses.'

- 'I don't know what today holds for me, Lord. I need your guidance, your advice. I need you to help me be alert. Direct my heart and thoughts to those words you know I need.'

- 'Lord, your Word is a mirror in which I often find myself. Show me myself here, as you see me, alone or with others. Thank you that you understand how I feel as I read your Word.'

- 'Lord, there are things here I don't understand. Please help me through the notes in this guide, or give me others who may help me.'

RESPOND Try to find a key thought or phrase which has come to you from this passage to carry with you through the day. Pray for people who are on your mind at the moment. Determine to share your experiences with others.

USING THIS GUIDE

Encounter through the Bible is a devotional Bible guide that can be used any time. It uses some of the best of the *Encounter with God* Bible series to guide the reader through whole Bible books in a systematic way. Like *Encounter with God*, it is designed for thinking Christians who want to interpret and apply the Bible in a way that is relevant to the problems and issues of today's world.

It is hoped that eventually the series will lead readers through the whole Bible. This volume covers Matthew and Mark. Look out for the other guides available now:

Old Testament
Genesis, Exodus, Leviticus
Numbers, Deuteronomy, Joshua
Judges, Ruth, 1 & 2 Samuel

New Testament
Luke, John

The notes are arranged in Bible book order – in this volume, Matthew and Mark. Each Bible book series begins with an introduction giving an overview of the book and its message. These aim to help you to get a grip on the book as a whole.

Each daily note begins with a call to worship which should help you consciously to come into God's presence before you read the passage. The main 'explore' section aims to bring out the riches hidden in the text. The response section at the end of the note may include praise or prayer and suggest ways of applying the message to daily living.

MATTHEW

Matthew, the first Gospel of the New Testament, tells of the birth, life, death and resurrection of Jesus. It was probably written between AD 50 and AD 90.

Matthew clearly wishes to show the connection between Jesus and the Old Testament and has a special interest in the fulfilment of Old Testament prophecy. The Gospel speaks of Jesus as King and the kingdom, and of the church fulfilling Israel's call to be a holy people and to show God to the world.

Whilst it was probably intended mainly for Jewish Christians, Matthew may also have been writing to persuade others that Jesus was the Messiah the Jews had expected for so long. The first two chapters, with their genealogical record and account of the nativity, show how the whole of the Old Testament was leading to Jesus, Christ the King.

Outline

1 The coming of the Messiah	1:1 – 4:25
2 The Sermon on the Mount	5:1 – 7:29
3 The preaching of the kingdom	8:1 – 9:38
4 The mission of the Twelve	10:1-42
5 The response of the people	11:1 – 12:50
6 The parables of the kingdom	13:1-58
7 The revealing of the Lord	14:1 – 17:27
8 The lifestyle of the church	18:1-35
9 The road to the cross	19:1 – 20:34
10 The days in Jerusalem	21:1 – 23:39
11 The shape of the future	24:1 – 25:46
12 The climax of his mission	26:1 – 28:20

'WORKING HIS PURPOSE OUT'[1]

'Though he was rich, yet for your sake he became poor, so that you through his poverty might become rich.'[2]

What is the point that Matthew is trying to make in beginning his Gospel in this apparently tedious way? His key concern is not so much 'What did Jesus do?' as 'Who is he?' Matthew's first readership was probably Jewish, and so he is saying to them, 'I want you to take seriously what he says because of who he is.' In tracing the genealogy from Abraham, he shows that Jesus was a true Jew; in taking his line through Judah to David, he is claiming that Jesus stands in the royal line, with a claim to the throne of David; and to help us to see that Jesus is the goal of the whole list, Matthew arranges the names into three groups of 14 names, or six groups of seven names – seven being a symbolic number, and Jesus being born as the climax of the whole list. So, Matthew says, this birth is the one Israel has been anticipating for many years, and is part of God's amazing plan. The hand of the Lord was there, preparing for the birth of the Messiah.

Matthew includes five women in the record (vs 3,5,6,16), which was not a normal thing to do in a genealogy. Some of these women seem strange choices (Tamar, who pretended to be a prostitute to make her father-in-law, Judah, recognise his ill-treatment of her; Rahab, a Canaanite prostitute; Ruth, a Moabitess; and Bathsheba, seduced by David).[3] God works in ways we don't expect, Matthew seems to be telling us, so watch out for what he's going to do now. Then he tells us that the Messiah is going to be born miraculously, and it's all part of God's amazing plan, foretold many years ago (v 23), as he rescues people (v 21) by coming to earth (v 23) and does things that might be regarded as inconceivable.

Ask God to show you ways in which he is working today, as he keeps his promises, fulfils his purposes and blesses those who trust him.

---

[1] AC Ainger, 1841–1919 [2] 2 Cor 8:9 [3] *See* Charles Price, *Matthew*, FOB; Christian Focus, 1998, p19–22, on the women in the genealogy

RECOGNISE THE KING!

'Thanks be to God for his indescribable gift!'[1]

MATTHEW 2

Although Matthew's Gospel was written with Jews especially in mind, he also wants to emphasise that Jesus, the King of the Jews, would bring God's peace and justice to the whole world.[2] And the first people to recognise who Jesus really was were Gentiles! These verses show how different people reacted to Jesus, reactions that are common in the rest of Matthew's Gospel.

Animosity and rejection: note how Herod responded to Jesus (vs 8,16). Any new 'King of the Jews' was a threat, and Herod, who willingly slaughtered members of his own family when he thought they were scheming against him, would think nothing of killing many babies to ensure that a royal pretender did not usurp his throne.

Mediocre indifference: the priests and teachers seemed aware of the Old Testament indication of where the Messiah would be born (vs 4–6), but they did not seem to be concerned to go further and seek him out for themselves. They could quote Scripture accurately, but were indifferent to its implications or its demand for a personal response.

Humble worship: the Magi 'bowed down and worshipped him. Then they opened their treasures' (v 11), having been 'overjoyed' (v 10). This is a good description of true worship – heartfelt, joyful and extravagant. Some take note of the actual gifts and suggest their significance: gold is the gift fit for a king – as Jesus was born to be; frankincense was used by priests in offerings – and here was the ultimate priest; and myrrh was used to embalm the dead – this baby was born to die. So these gifts tell us who Jesus is, what he came to do and what it cost him. Who would not bow in wonder before a God who loves us that much!

John Newton once wrote in a sermon script, 'Jesus Christ is precious!' How precious is Jesus to us?

[1] 2 Cor 9:15 [2] *See, eg,* Isa 11:1–10

WHEN GOD COMES TO CALL…

'A warning of judgement, but also an invitation to life and change.'[1]

'God is coming back, and he's going to bring comfort and rescue. It's time to get ready!' That was the message John the Baptist brought the people. That had been the message to the Jewish people since Isaiah first exclaimed it,[2] but the people weren't ready, even though preparing for the coming King was the 'obsessive centre'[3] of Isaiah's vision.

John was anticipating an entirely new order (vs 9–11). His message to the establishment was that there was no security in what they were by birth. Religious pedigree does not mean a guaranteed part in God's kingdom. There was to be a new relationship, a new dimension. The prophets had said God would come when his people turned back to him wholeheartedly. This is what many now came to do (vs 5,6), as they responded to John's message.

Verses 2 and 8 provide a succinct summary of what is needed to live in God's kingdom, as well as how to prepare for its coming. There is to be a radical changing of the mind. It's not enough merely to feel bad about our sin. 'As we think in our heart, so we are.'[4] Confession is to lead to action. There is to be fruit to demonstrate reality. There is to be sharing, honesty and contentment, to show change in our daily lives. This is how John expresses it in Luke 3:8–14. There are to be practical expressions of our repentance. And we are to respond like this because of the kingship of Christ. Our response is to recognise who he is and submit to his kingship, so that the agenda and interests of his kingdom become the focus of our lives. To enable us to live like this, we need the life-giving Spirit of God to cleanse and empower us (v 11).

Lord, open my heart to live in sincerity before you and experience your ministry in my life, humbly dependent on your Spirit.

---

[1] MJ Wilkins, *Matthew*, NIVAC; Zondervan, 2004, p148 [2] Isa 40 [3] M Green, *Matthew for Today*, Hodder & Stoughton, 1988, p56 [4] Prov 23:7, AV (adapted)

SURPRISED BY JESUS!

'Jesus ... being in very nature God ... made himself nothing ... being made in human likeness.'[1]

MATTHEW 3:13–17

Jesus is the King! He's the Creator and Ruler of the universe.[2] He's the great Judge.[3] John recognised who Jesus was (v 14) and so tried to deter him from being baptised – this was the person who would do all John spoke of in verses 11 and 12. Baptism is for those who have repented – and Jesus doesn't need to repent! So why does Jesus ask John to baptise him?

Verse 15 gives Jesus' reason. But how is 'all righteousness' being fulfilled in this way? Perhaps a key aspect here is that of Jesus humbly classifying himself with his people, by taking their place, and identifying with their need for cleansing. He 'was numbered with the transgressors'.[4] Perhaps also 'righteousness' here refers to that quality of life that those being baptised were to demonstrate, which John himself lived and demanded of his followers.[5] Jesus was recognising God's claim on him, as on his followers, for obedience and holiness. Moreover, John is here publicly announcing the arrival of the Messiah and the start of his ministry. This in itself was a profound anticipation of his 'baptism' on the cross, as Mark 10:38 puts it. Here is an advanced symbolic demonstration of what will be Jesus' experience.

How will this bring about what John was expecting: judgement and restoration for God's people? Perhaps Matthew would say, 'Read the rest of my Gospel to find out'! As Jesus comes out of the water, receives God's Spirit in a new way, and is called God's Son who brings the Father great joy, maybe he is saying that his judgement is through the making of peace by suffering on the cross. This may not be what Jews of the first century expected,[6] but Jesus often acts in ways which are unexpected and surprising.

How can we learn anew to be surprised by Jesus – 'humble', 'peaceful', 'obedient', 'dependent on God'? May our disposition to God and to others reflect his attitude.

[1] Phil 2:5–7 [2] John 1:1–3 [3] John 5:30 [4] Isa 53:12 [5] Matt 21:32 [6] Cf 1 Cor 1:23

SUSTAINED BY GOD'S WORD

God's voice welcomes us as his children, but we also hear the whispered suggestions of the enemy...

MATTHEW 4:1–11

Jesus has just had a spiritual high at his baptism. After such a great experience, temptation often follows. 'It can sort out the emotional high from the reality of spiritual conquest and growth.'[1] How are we daily to live our Christian lives? How does God want to bless us and help us to build spiritual muscles for whatever challenges face us? How does Satan attempt to sidetrack us and get us to go contrary to the Father's will (as he tries to do with Jesus here)?

God uses Satan's designs to a good purpose. Jesus is here actually strengthened for his messianic role through his battle with the devil. God is in control of both the tempter and the circumstances (the Spirit led Jesus to be tempted, v 1), and he will never allow a believer to be tempted beyond what he or she is able to endure.[2]

There is a uniqueness to the temptations of Jesus, and we should see allusions to the fall of Adam and the wanderings of Israel in the wilderness. Jesus, as the unique Son of God, has as his mission to put right the previous failures, and is also the prototype of victory for all who follow him.[3] Jesus' quotations from Deuteronomy[4] perhaps indicate that he had been reading from this book in his own devotions. The Spirit takes this word of God and uses it in spiritual warfare. I must ask myself, how well do I feed on the Scriptures, to be alert to the Spirit and share Jesus' victory? Do I trust the Spirit and use his methods in warfare against the devil? Let us beware of the temptations of building our own kingdoms, looking for personal gratification and compromising with Satan, and rather follow Jesus' method of gaining victory!

What enticing whispers echo around your head, tempting you to turn from what God wants you to do and be? Use the same defences as Jesus to defeat the enemy!

---

[1] M Green, *Matthew for Today*, p63 [2] 1 Cor 10:13 assures us of this [3] Heb 4:14–16 [4] Deut 8:3; 6:13,16

LEAVING ALL FOR JESUS

'My Jesus, my Saviour, / Lord, there is none like you. / All of my days, I want to praise, / the wonders of your mighty love.'[1]

MATTHEW 4:12–25

'Jesus was universal enough to include both Jews and Gentiles in his messianic gospel, authoritative enough to transform simple men into leaders of a movement that changed the course of history, and effective enough to attend to the basic needs of the people – body, soul and spirit.'[2] This quotation sums up perceptively what is going on in these 14 verses!

Jesus starts in a place described as a land of darkness. The province of Galilee was not large but was densely populated; it was an area that Jews looked down upon – derided as 'Galilee of the Gentiles' (v 15). So Jesus has started his ministry in the sort of place where the orthodox would never have expected to find him, among crowds who lived alongside pagans. The light he brings reaches to all. Note his message: the kingly rule of heaven is approaching – so get ready, stop what you are doing, and do the opposite instead (v 17)! Four fishermen immediately respond to this (vs 18–22).

If we want to know more specifically what the gospel of the kingdom is, verses 23–25 tell us. Jesus' ministry involved three aspects: teaching, preaching the kingdom, and healing. He informed the mind with a view to changing the will, as someone once summed up teaching. He proclaimed the arrival of God's reign. He also healed every kind of illness: this aspect of kingdom ministry is sometimes sidelined, but the church's role today is to embrace all three of these strands of ministry. Jesus Christ is interested in the whole person. These healings were signs of the new thing that God was doing through Jesus. In his person, he had a dynamism that attracted many people. He is someone worth sacrificing our lives for.

How are we working to extend God's kingdom in the world? Are Jesus' priorities those that we hold dear? Are we presenting him as wonderful, loving and sovereign?

[1] Darlene Zschech © 1993 Hillsongs Australia [2] Michael J Wilkins, *Matthew*, p171

UNLUCKY FOR SOME…

'Leave empty things to empty-minded people, and direct your thought to God's commands for you. Shut the door upon yourself, and invite in Jesus your beloved.'[1]

MATTHEW 5:1–12

Nine times in this brief passage the word 'blessed' is used. We struggle to find an accurate translation for the Greek – *makarios* – because it carries a concept better understood in the ancient world than in our own. Some versions use 'happy', but this doesn't quite capture it – 'happy' implies an inner, emotional state, whereas 'blessed' is an outward, objective condition. We can't use 'fortunate' because it is not by good fortune alone that these people have benefited; likewise, 'lucky' doesn't cut it. 'Blessed' implies one who blesses; to be blessed is to have received from one who has the power to give. The 'blessed' are those who have received from God, or are in a position to receive, all that he has to give them. Who are the real winners in the race for significance and satisfaction? Those who know that it is from the hand of God that all good things come.

And, according to Jesus, they are not the usual suspects. This is no list of the well-to-do. Rather it is the poor, the hungry, the bereaved, the meek and merciful (vs 3–7) who enter the winners' enclosure. Where every culture in history has pandered to power and made royalty of the rich, the kingdom that Jesus proclaims (vs 3,10) will instead bring good news to the humble poor. From the outset, Jesus wants to make one thing clear. The trinkets that make winners of their owners in this world will have no currency in the new kingdom. It is those the world has laughed at as losers who will find themselves winning beyond their wildest dreams. The Hebrew term for the humble poor – *anawim* – describes people whose poverty has made them deeply reliant on God. If the roll call of anawim were called today, would your name appear?

Jesus urges us to rejoice and be glad even when we are slandered, insulted and persecuted (v 12). Pray for an explosion of such joy, even in the most difficult of times.

---

1 Thomas à Kempis, *The Imitation of Christ*, English translation, Fontana, 1963

LIVING ON PURPOSE

'Lord, grant me ... that my lamp may feel thy kindling touch and know no quenching; may burn for me and for others may give light.'[1]

MATTHEW 5:13–16

These famous words, in which we are called to be salt and light in the world, are the very heart of Jesus' sermon. They are often misunderstood as a simple call to be more effective in Christian witness, but in reality they go deeper. They are in effect an evangelistic call to all who might hear them to rediscover, in relationship with Christ, the purpose for which they were created. Human beings have been made to be salt and light in God's world, and the followers of Christ are invited to rediscover and re-enter that task. From Genesis onwards, women and men have been called to be God's image-bearers in the world; to rule over it as he would; to preserve the good and bring out the flavours locked up within it. To be human, Jesus says, is to have a purpose. Every gift we have been granted has been given to this end. Our intelligence and artistry; our creativity and character; our strength and stamina: all these have been given to us so that we can work in partnership with God to unlock the full potential of his garden.

How tragic, given such a task, that we should lose our way; that the God-flavours of our lives should be diluted (v 13). How terrible to be called to be a caretaker and end up as a vandal. The discourse of Jesus is nothing less than a call to return to our first purposes, to recover the miracle and the magnificence of God's intentions for humanity. To follow Christ, to respond to his mountainside call, is to rediscover in the deepest possible sense why we're alive. In the great adventure of following Christ, we become, once more, salt to the earth. The light of our God-given gifts is able to shine once more. Alone and together (v 16), we become a shining beacon of our Creator's love and grace.

How will your local streets, workplaces or communities experience the taste of God's love if the salt stays safely in the saltshaker? God has given you both light and flavour: spread them!

[1] Prayer of Columbanus, Irish monk and missionary, AD 543–615

INNER TRANSFORMATION

'The core of Christian revelation is that Jesus Christ is the sole legitimate Lord of all human lives.'[1]

MATTHEW 5:17–26

Jesus' claim to be the fulfilment of the Law has caused great confusion. To the religious leaders of his own day, it was a deeply offensive claim. They were experts in the Law: for them it was the highest expression of the purposes and character of God – much as Islamic law is to Muslims today. By suggesting (v 17) that he could 'fulfil' the Law, Jesus was implying that it was not, on its own, enough: that it was an incomplete expression of God's best. Others have taken this as an excuse to abandon adherence to the Law altogether and, for that matter, to any law. Some of the earliest Christians fell into this trap of interpreting 'freedom in Christ' as freedom from every moral constraint.[2] But this is not what Jesus is proposing.

What he is saying is that he will achieve in his incarnation what the Law could never achieve. He will make it possible for us to obey. He will do this not by piling on greater and greater constraints, nor by refining the Law's demands down to microscopic detail. Rather, he will take on the law of death itself in unarmed combat, defeat the power of sin and make it possible for the Spirit of God – the very character of God himself – to enter into the human heart. Jesus himself will become the fulfilment that the Law could never be. Law can only deal with the outward manifestations of sin and decay: it is a damage-limitation strategy, containing the effects of sin until the root cause can be dealt with. The law can limit murder (v 21) but it cannot heal the angry heart (v 22). Jesus promises to go beyond containment to the very cause, the very root of our inability to obey (15:16-20), and to make good our rebellious hearts (5:8; 22:37).

Jesus goes right to the heart: to attitudes, intentions and inner transformation. Don't struggle to obey in your own strength. Let Jesus, fulfilment of the Law, transform your heart.

---

1 H Kraemer, Dutch Reformed missiologist, 1888–1965 **2** Gal 5:13

RECLAIM YOUR HEART

'Christians are not meant to just try and do good, be nice and help the world work a little better. They are instead to act as signposts to ... another way of life, another kingdom'.[1]

MATTHEW 5:27–37

This is a great passage to show to those who have left the church because they think the Jesus we worship is too soft and unreal. There is little sign here of the 'gentle Jesus, meek and mild' who is too innocent and naive to help us in the darker corners of our lives. This is Jesus being blunt, frank and even explicit about the workings of temptation in our lives. If this graphic passage could be summed up in just three words, they would be these: take sin seriously.

Jesus doesn't want to embarrass his listeners by openly listing their sins, but he does want them to know that he understands. He is the same flesh and blood as you or I. He knows what goes on in the minds and hearts of humanity. And he knows that sometimes something radical is needed to break us free from the temptations that so easily entangle us. 'Take the necessary action', he insists; take seriously the messages that your fantasies are sending. Were he speaking in a twenty-first-century mall, rather than on a first-century mountainside, what radical action might he call for? Might he suggest that those consumed by the pornographic enticements of the internet take action by selling their computer? Might he urge those easily drawn into dishonesty, or whose temper often flares, to forge accountable relationships? Instead of suggesting you cut off your right hand, might he ask you to cut in half your credit card? Using illustrations of marriage, divorce (v 31) and oath-taking (v 33), he establishes a demanding standard of honesty and integrity. Wherever money, sex or power – the 'big three' temptations of human society – gain control of us, something is lost. Take the necessary action. Reclaim your own heart and mind for Christ.

Open up to God about your secret struggles. Prayerfully and honestly, note the areas that are 'dark corners' in your heart. Pray for grace, wisdom and strength as you take action.

[1] Graham Tomlin, *The Provocative Church*, SPCK, 2002

HOW FAR WOULD JESUS GO?

'The key, then, to loving God is to see Jesus, to hold him before the mind with as much fullness and clarity as possible.'[1]

MATTHEW 5:38–48

Revenge is one of the most powerful of all human instincts. Wars have been sparked, great novels written and epic films made, based on the need, when evil is done, to pay it back. 'Don't get mad, get even', we urge one another, as we make heroes of those who mete out summary justice to evil men. Such was the hunger for revenge in Israel's history that laws were set to limit the level of justice demanded, so that punishment was commensurate with the crime. These are the laws that Jesus is citing here.[2] They were intended to limit, not excuse or glorify revenge. But even that is not enough for Jesus. He wants us to go further, deeper. He is proposing a radically different approach. He is not content just to limit the cycle of violence and counter-violence: he wants to break it altogether (v 39). This is about more than justice – it is about mercy. It is about giving to those who have taken from us (v 40); about the victim taking the initiative to serve (v 41). Jesus gives power to the powerless, because even the most victimised person has the power to forgive.

Two characteristics mark this love that Jesus is asking us to show, even to our enemies (v 44). The first is that it goes beyond our normal expectations (v 46). Where I might normally insist on my rights it tells me, instead, to pay heed to my responsibilities. Where I might look for revenge and restitution, it tells me instead to hold out for redemption. The second characteristic is that it is an active love. This is no passive acceptance of evil. We are called to love actively (v 44), to target our love where it is most needed (v 46) and to pray for those who are against us. It is a high and lofty call, modelled on the perfect love of God himself (v 48), and the miracle is that Jesus makes it possible.

These verses are perhaps the best commentary on the question, 'What would Jesus do?' He asks nothing that he himself would not do. What challenges do you face where Jesus' example can show you how to act?

---

[1] Dallas Willard, *The Divine Conspiracy*, HarperCollins, 1998 [2] Exod 21:24; Lev 24:19,20; Deut 19:21

FOR GOD'S EYES ONLY

A prominent Hindu once said that he would believe in Christ if Christians only looked a little more saved. 'Change my heart, O God.'

MATTHEW 6:1–8

There is a subtle shifting of gear between chapters 5 and 6 of Matthew, suggesting that Jesus is turning a corner from the what and why of Christian discipleship to the how. In Chapter 5, Jesus has outlined the ways of 'right living' that he urges his followers to adopt. The 'righteousness' described here (v 1) is the same as that introduced in 5:20, where the disciples are asked to outclass the Pharisees themselves in their obedience. Jesus has shown just how high the standard is; just how radical he is asking his followers to be. But the danger, once they have this knowledge, is that they themselves will become like the Pharisees: that they will use all that Jesus has given them to put on a great display of religious achievement. Jesus fears that they will turn right living into a public performance. Even the most loving, the most selfless, the most radical religion in the world can be turned, in the wrong hands, into hypocrisy.

So Jesus asks for a right living that is 'for God's eyes only'. He asks us to behave rightly, not to earn social kudos, but to please our Heavenly Father. 'Your Father … sees what is done in secret,' he says twice (vs 4,6), he 'knows what you need' (v 8). At the heart of these demands is the wonderful truth that Christian obedience is not religious observance – it is the joyful outworking of a love-relationship with God. At the heart of Christianity is relationship. Take that away and you are left with the dried husk of hypocrisy. Make it central, and you have the joyful union of creature and Creator. Jesus establishes that piety is personal, not public, and asks us to trade earth's applause for heaven's favour. And what is the 'reward' he speaks of (vs 4,6)? It is to know God more; to spend more time with him; to know that he is with us and loves us. Relationship with God, in this sense, is its own reward.

What marks the difference between religion and relationship with God? How might you move more deeply from the first to the second?

(FOR)GIVE US THIS DAY...

'Lead us from the unreal to the real. Lead us from darkness to light. Lead us from death to immortality.'[1]

MATTHEW 6:9–18

Having established that true Christian piety is founded on a love-relationship with the Father, Jesus goes on to offer a model for the content and character of prayer. In one sense he offers this as 'a prayer', so that 'The Lord's Prayer' has become a central pillar of devotion throughout history and across the world. But in another sense it is a model for all prayer: a window into everything that prayer should be. These brief verses point us to why we pray; what we might pray for; and what might happen when we do.

The *why* of prayer is grounded in the nature of God – who he is, where he is and what he is doing. God is the accessible and approachable Father (v 9), who has an eagle's-eye view of every need and circumstance we face. Nothing is mysterious to him. And he is in the business of bringing to this earth on which we live the blessings and the joys of heaven (v 10).

The *what* of prayer encompasses the things we need everyday. We need to see provision for our everyday essentials (v 11). This is more than bread alone – it is all that we need to make it through the day (see 4:4). And we need the power of forgiveness to heal the broken places in and around us (v 12). This is a dual power, as cyclical as breathing: the power both to give and to receive.

The *what if* of prayer is the guidance and protection of God (v 13). As we learn to walk with him as Father, in free and open communion, we will know his guiding hand; we will be led not into trial and temptation but into life; we will be protected and we will, ultimately, be delivered from the very presence and possibility of evil. Now that is a goal worth praying for and a joy worth fasting for!

This prayer implies daily use, since it mentions 'daily bread'. How might it change your life if you asked God daily where you need forgiveness – and whom you should forgive?

---

[1] A prayer from India

TAKE 'THE JESUS QUIZ'

'If God can do more than you can imagine, why not ask for more imagination?'[1]

MATTHEW 6:19–34

Having set out a pattern of prayer that points towards simple, daily dependence on the Father, Jesus understands that issues will be raised for his hearers. What about my possessions; my goals; my money? What about the future? All these things weigh heavy on me. I have responsibilities. How can I live in simple trust when there is, frankly, so much to worry over? Jesus suggests a kind of spiritual health-check to point his hearers to a better way of living – a quiz with four questions: What are you investing in (vs 19,20)? What have you set your sights on (vs 22,23)? Whom are you serving (v 24)? What keeps you awake at night (v 25)?

Each of these touches on an area that for many of us will be a raw nerve. The things we invest in will so often become the things that draw our hearts. What is it for you: property and possessions or the priority of God's will in your life? The things we set our sights on, too, will shape our actions. Where your eyes linger, your mind and body will soon follow. What is it for you: the glossy promises of a thousand coloured adverts, or the simple goals of the purposes of God? Whom we serve will also dictate our direction. Who's your boss: cash, or your Creator? And the things that bring anxiety to us will, more often than not, tell us where our hearts are truly headed. What fills your mind as you lay your head on the pillow each night: your own needs, or the grace and glories of God?

The Jesus-prescription for each of these areas is the same: it is the kingdom (v 33). Invest in the kingdom. Set your sights on the kingdom. Serve the kingdom. Let the kingdom fill your mind. Here is the Jesus way (v 34): put God first, and sleep in peace.

Take a few moments with a blank piece of paper to complete 'The Jesus Quiz' for your own life. Consider the questions above, and jot down the thoughts they spark in you; take some time to pray about your answers.

[1] Dan Davidson, 'mission mobiliser' and writer, from *God's Great Ambition*, Gabriel Books, 2003

AMATEUR OPTICIANS

'O Lord God, Creator of all. Open my eye to beauty. Open my mind to wonder. Open my ears to others. Open my heart to you.'[1]

Having told us so emphatically not to worry, Jesus now instructs us not to judge (v 1). These seem to be two very different ideas, but in fact they are closely linked, because they both spring from the same root. They are both fruits of our inability, or refusal, to trust.

When we worry, it is because we can't trust God to bring us to the place we long to be. When we judge, it is almost the same problem. Unwilling to allow God sovereignty over the lives of others, we impose our own rule, with our own ideas about how they should behave, and how fast they should be showing the fruits of grace. Jesus' cartoon-like image (vs 3,4) shows us that not only is it wrong to stare into your brother's eye trying to locate his speck of failure, it is also impossible, when out of your own eye there protrudes a six-foot floorboard. You are hardly equipped for optical microsurgery when you can't turn your head without breaking something! No, says Jesus, stop telling others how to live and start asking God how you should live (v 5). If you believe there are high standards to aspire to, aspire to them yourself. Commit yourself to God's tender care and have the grace and wisdom to do the same for others.

Shifting the imagery from planks and specks to pigs, dogs and jewels (v 6), Jesus is perhaps amplifying the warning against interfering in others' lives. The right time to offer help to others is when they are ready to receive it. Offer it to those who like wild dogs and pigs are untamed, and you will reap only anger and rejection.[2] Don't appoint yourself as judge over those who have not invited it. Let go, and let God be their judge.

Are there people you find it hard to leave to God? Ask God to give you the courage to release them, and the grace and wisdom to help when asked.

---

[1] David Adam, *Power Lines*, 1992   [2] Prov 9:8

THE POWER OF ACTIVE LOVE

'What is our life on earth, if not discovering, becoming conscious of, penetrating, contemplating, accepting, loving this mystery of God, the unique reality which surrounds us, and in which we are immersed like meteorites in space?'[1]

MATTHEW 7:7–12

Having hinted strongly that worry and judgement are both issues of trust, Jesus now moves on to make the hint explicit. The alternative to a lifestyle of anxiety consumed by fear of nakedness and hunger – and likewise to a life of cruel criticism in which we lunge at every sawdust speck with planks of judgement – is a relationship of trust with our Creator. In both cases the negative emotion is replaced, not by empty neutrality but by energetic engagement. The opposite of worry is not an absence of anxiety but the presence of God. The opposite of judgement is not indifference but love. Three actions are at the heart of this. We are to ask, to seek and to knock (v 7), and it is those who do these things (v 8) who find what they are looking for. Doing nothing is not an option. We are called to active love.

Jesus perhaps senses that there is a danger in the words he has just spoken. He has promised that all who ask, seek and knock will receive, find and be given entry. Doesn't this turn God into a cosmic blessing-machine waiting only for us to drop the coins of prayer into the right slot? Is the sovereign God obliged to do our bidding? Jesus addresses this false possibility by taking us back to relationship, to the image of child and parent (vs 9-11). God gives to us not because he must, but because he wants to. He is a caring parent, not a machine. Take Jesus seriously, if you have children (v 9). Now multiply that feeling by ten, by a hundred, by a thousand. Can you begin to feel how God feels about you? And can you hear the hidden challenge, that this is how you, too, should feel for others (v 12)?

This sums up the law and the prophets, Jesus says. This is the heart of the message. You have been on the receiving end of grace – now put yourself on the giving end.[2]

---

[1] Carlo Carretto, Catholic hermit, 1910–88 [2] Matt 10:8b

GATES AND ROADS

'Nobody climbs a mountain pulling a trailer behind them. To move on and up in Godzone, you have to learn to let go ... To grasp, to cling, to hold on: these come naturally. To let go without being forced to is to share in the life of God.'[1]

MATTHEW 7:13–20

Three images sit side by side in this brief passage to illustrate for us the realities of the life to which Jesus calls us. Together, they tell us that becoming more like God won't be easy – and it won't be quick.

The idea of a small gate and a narrow road are simple images of a hard journey. To get through a small gate, you may have to untie whatever burden you are carrying; you may have to pass your belongings through one by one. You may even have to leave some things behind. Another image springs to mind, of a camel trying to get through the eye of the needle (19:24).[2] You have to be small and humble and empty-handed to pass unhindered through this gate. Children, for example, find it easy (18:2–4). There is a twin implication here of relinquishment and determination – of laying aside every weight that might hold you back from God's way, and pressing on to make a way through. The wide and narrow gates lead to different roads: a broad (easy) road or a narrow (hard) one (vs 13,14). The narrow road is harder to find. It is less travelled; less obvious; less clearly marked. Others might urge you to take the better-known way, but if you want to walk the Jesus way, you must be firm in your resolve to find it.

The Jesus way is also slow. You can't 'fake' transformation, like a wolf pulling on the costume of a sheep (v 15). There is no shop-bought substitute for the hard work of holiness. The only results that matter are the fruit you bear (v 16); the genuine, long-term outworking of your inner identity. You can't fake fruit (v 17), nor short-circuit the time it takes to grow. It has its own pace and process. And it tells you everything you need to know (v 20) about the health and strength of the tree on which it grows.

Don't try to fool God with a shop-bought 'costume' of holiness. Go for the real thing; take the time to let the real fruit grow.

[1] Mike Riddell, *Godzone*, Lion, 1998 [2] Mark 10:25; Luke 18:25

ATTITUDE IS EVERYTHING

'Faith is something you are ready to die for. Doctrine is something you're prepared to kill for. There is a world of difference between the two.'[1]

MATTHEW 7:21–29

Not all faith is the true faith Jesus is asking for. Not all religion is the true piety he seeks (v 21). To paraphrase, 'It ain't what you do, it's the way that you do it'. It is possible to have the form of religion – to do and say what seem to be all the right things – and yet not have the reality within (vs 22,23). The test is whether we 'do the will of [the] Father' (v 21). The implication here (vs 21–23) is that there are people who have prophesied, cast out demons and performed miracles without ever knowing if this was God's will in the situation. They are trying to please God without asking God's opinion on the matter.

Once again, Jesus places an active love-relationship at the very heart of Christian religion. For how can we know God's will, unless we know God? To know what God wants in each situation we face implies a deep devotional life; that we will ask God so often what he wants that we start to know by instinct; that we are so familiar with the person of God that it becomes easy to recognise his purposes. Only those who have this relationship can dare to do what God requires.

Those Jesus commends, by contrast, are those who both hear and do God's will (v 24). From a relationship of active love, they hear what God is saying: from a heart of willing obedience, they do it. Theirs is wisdom of a careful builder, anchoring everything on strong foundations. No storm can flatten a life anchored in such active love (v 25). To build without it is, quite simply, disastrous (v 27). The house built on such a relationship is strong, secure and lasting. The house built on any other foundation falls flat. Little wonder the crowds were in awe (v 28), stunned by the sheer authority of Jesus' words. Here is one of the most graphic and compelling contrasts painted in Scripture.

Consider the foundations of your Christian beliefs and practices. Are they 'built on' a relationship of active love: a deep and daily life of devotion? Talk to God about this.

[1] Tony Benn, British Labour politician, 1925–

FAITH IN SURPRISING PLACES

Dear Lord, please teach me through today's reading more about what pleases you, and help me to please you more.

Matthew introduces us to the theme of healing with two stories, the first of which relates to a man with leprosy, a common condition in first-century Judea. What is important to Matthew's Jewish readers is the recognition that such diseases resulted in the person being marginalised from communal and religious life.[1] Furthermore, they were associated with judgement for personal sin.[2]

These men needed not just physical restoration but also restoration to their community and to God. It is no accident that Matthew records that Jesus touches the man, even stretching to do so (v 3). Touching the sick was a very unusual act for a Jew because of the fear of ceremonial contamination. Jesus, however, regularly incorporated it into his healings. By touching the untouchable, Jesus demonstrates his authority over the Law as well as his ability to bring healing without being tainted by the disease. The story also reveals Jesus' determination to reintegrate the man into society. Jesus' touch shows his authority, an authority that demands obedience on the part of the man (v 4).

The second healing takes place at a distance, without any apparent evidence to support the centurion's assumption that Jesus could act like this. Somehow he had become convinced that Jesus was able to do the impossible. Is our faith limited by what we have already seen Jesus do or are we open to new possibilities? While the man with the skin disease recognised that Jesus had power to heal, the centurion realised that Jesus' power was delegated to him from a superior source. Reading stories of God at work can increase our appreciation of the authority and awesome power Jesus exercises, and encourage us to trust him more both for our personal circumstances and for the wider issues that concern us.

Lord, help me to be more aware of your authority, to listen to you more readily and to explore your splendour more eagerly.

[1] Lev 13:45,46 [2] Num 12:9–15

THE HEART OF DISCIPLESHIP

Lord, help me follow you today in a way that truly pleases you. Teach me more about being your follower from this reading.

MATTHEW 8:14–22

This story of the restoration of Peter's mother-in-law from a fever is the third healing miracle recorded by Matthew. Here we see Jesus taking the initiative in the healing process and touching her. He is the one in charge, there being no mention of the disciples in Matthew's account. Jesus has no regard for the rabbinic rule that one should not touch a person with a fever for fear that one might be ceremonially contaminated. The healing is enacted without any word from Jesus: the fever is removed by his simple touch (v 15).

Mark and Luke note that after she had been healed, Peter's mother-in-law served the group, indicating her complete recovery.[1] Matthew, however, prefers to keep the focus on Jesus, informing us that she served him. She is presented as the ideal disciple who responds to a touch from Jesus by ministering to him. As we think of occasions when the Lord has blessed us recently we may ask ourselves whether or not this has moved us to serve him in some way – perhaps by serving his needy brethren.[2] Jesus' authority is demonstrated by his ability to heal everyone who was brought to him (v 16).

In contrast to the response of service shown by Peter's mother-in-law, verses 18–22 record the excuses offered by people who indicated a desire to follow Jesus but who did not make a practical response. Even though Matthew demonstrates that Jesus' healings show him to be the promised Messiah, some prefer not to follow him. Today, as then, following Jesus carries a cost. It is important to check regularly the quality of our discipleship. Disciples are determined by their service to Jesus. The challenge to us is whether we will serve Jesus or make excuses. Are we willing to learn from Jesus' attitudes, priorities and values, or are we too obsessed with our own agendas?

Lord, thank you for calling me to follow you. Help me to be a better disciple, especially as regards the issues you are challenging me about.

---

[1] Mark 1:31; Luke 4:39 [2] Matt 25:37–40

PEACE IN A STORM

Lord help me to know your peace in my storms and to realise afresh that I am safe because you are with me.

MATTHEW 8:23–27

Generally, the Jews were not great seafarers and the prospect of travelling on water filled the normal Jew with fear. Lake Galilee, some 200 metres below sea level and surrounded by mountains, often experienced rapidly developing fierce storms. Despite some of the disciples being experienced fishermen, this storm exhibited an unusual ferocity and they feared they might drown. Their readiness to follow Jesus looked as if it might have been rash; but Matthew wants his readers to learn an important lesson: following Jesus is always right, even though circumstances may appear to indicate otherwise. Matthew develops the tension in the story by recording that Jesus is asleep. The disciples assume that this is because he doesn't care for them. Sometimes we fear that Jesus may be unaware of our situation or not care about the storms affecting our lives, but he is always there with us. The challenge is to develop our ability to trust him and to believe that he is in control of the storm and of us.

Thus far, Matthew has revealed Jesus healing people and expelling demons, but the calming of the storm demonstrates his authority to direct nature. Only God has the authority to supervise creation since he is the Creator. Jesus' action indicates that he has the authority of God himself. Thus the disciples have the opportunity to recognise that Jesus is not just a healer, not just the promised Messiah, but God incarnate. The one who promises to be always with us is not an angel or simply someone with supernatural power. He is God and he is committed to being with us.[1] The presence of storms does not indicate the absence of the Saviour;[2] Jesus was in the storm with the disciples and called 'time!' when they could take no more - as he will for us too.

Bring to God Christians who are suffering intensely for their faith in Muslim or communist countries and elsewhere. Pray that they may know the Lord's protecting and reassuring presence.

[1] Matt 28:20; Heb 13:5,6 [2] John 16:33

WHO HAS DOMINION OVER EVIL?

Lord, may this reading encourage me to understand more of your supreme authority. Thank you that no one is a threat to you.

MATTHEW 8:28–34

This is the first exorcism story recorded by Matthew. He concentrates again on the authority of Jesus, demonstrated by the ease with which he deals with the demons who dominated the lives of these two men. Despite their questions and their attempt to bargain with him, Jesus dismisses the demons with a word. They cannot help but acknowledge the supremacy of Jesus. In an insecure world in which life often appears to be fragile, and evil triumphant, it's important for us to remind ourselves who is actually in control. What circumstances are currently causing you concern? Remember that the Lord is never fazed by situations and we are never outside his supervising care.[1]

Even when it seems that the demons manipulated Jesus to do what they wanted him to do, namely to send them into the swine, we should not overlook evidence of the authority of Jesus. The demons did not choose to go of their own accord; they went because Jesus sent them. More importantly, when the swine leapt into the sea, they drowned. Not only was this clear evidence to the demoniacs that they were free of their unwelcome guests, but a truly powerful manifestation of the authority of Jesus was being played out in front of their eyes. To Jews, water signalled the demise of demons, and when the swine entered the water, they understood that Jesus had permanently terminated the demons' rule of terror. People today trapped by involvement in the occult or idolatry often benefit from a similar demonstration of Jesus' power. In what ways do you see the power of evil at work in your society? Never let the devil try to convince you that he will have the last word in your society's future or in your personal circumstances. Jesus is the victor![2]

Lord, thank you for your incredible authority. Help me to recognise it more, so that I can be stronger when the devil's lies seem so convincing.

[1] Gen 28:15; Deut 32:10; Rom 8:28,29 [2] Prov 21:30,31; 1 Cor 15:54–58; Col 2:15; 1 John 3:8

JESUS: SAVIOUR, HEALER OR BOTH?

Have you ever wondered whether Jesus can really forgive all your sins? Claim the promise in 1 John 1:9 once more.

MATTHEW 9:1–8

This is the sixth miracle recorded by Matthew, and once again it reveals the supremacy of Jesus. In this story, the ability of Jesus to forgive sins is highlighted. As far as the Jews were concerned, only God could forgive sins, so the religious leaders have a conundrum on their hands. They are aware that Jesus has significant powers and that his authority indicates that he may be the promised Messiah. However, now he does what no one, not even the Messiah, was expected to do – he pronounces forgiveness of sins. The paralytic maybe hoped for physical healing, but he received much more.

Because Jesus healed the paralytic, it appeared that his claim to forgive sins must be true because of the Jewish assumption that sickness was caused by personal sin. To provide healing indicated that the underlying cause must also have been resolved. However, another question in their minds was prompted by their assumption that God sent the sickness in the first place; so the healing indicated that Jesus had superseded an act of God – and despite there being no indication that the paralytic had confessed any sins, Jesus still pronounced forgiveness.

The fact that Jesus not only easily removes the man's paralysis but also removes his sin, his greater need, sets the stage for the people (and us) to recognise how uniquely special Jesus is. No problem, no sin, is outside the authority and power of the Lord.[1] Many times, we feel unforgivable and we wonder, 'Can Jesus forgive us again?' His willingness to forgive reveals God's love for sinners like us[2] – and for the socially marginalised we often ignore.[3]

Knowing we're forgiven helps us relax and also keeps us in awe of Jesus, our Saviour. Who could you share this with?

---

[1] Matt 28:18 [2] Mark 3:28; Luke 22:31,32; Rom 5:8; 8:34,35 [3] Luke 5:30–32; 15:1,20–24

FRIEND OF SINNERS

Take a moment to wonder that God brought you into his family. 'Father, thank you for adopting me as one of your beloved children.'

MATTHEW 9:9–13

Matthew loves to show the varied responses of people to Jesus. Here, he records his own reaction to the call of Jesus when he was a tax collector. In working for the oppressive, pagan force of Rome, tax collectors were regarded as traitors to their own Jewish communities; they were also notoriously corrupt and cruel. It's little wonder that tax collectors were identified with 'sinners' (v 10). Normal Jews kept well away from such disreputable people. Yet Jesus calls Matthew to follow him, and he immediately does so; the call of Jesus supersedes all sense of unworthiness he might have felt. However we may feel about ourselves, God demonstrates his affection for us in calling us to be members of his family.[1] When you feel such a sinner, remember that your sin didn't put Jesus off bringing you into God's family!

Matthew also records that Jesus eats with such people. For Jews, to eat with another indicated a measure of acceptance of their lifestyle. Consequently, some people were always excluded from their fellowship and friendship. The Pharisees were truly shocked by Jesus' openness. Jesus demonstrates not only that he is not contaminated by the sins of those with whom he eats but that it is a priority for him to be there with them. Do we make it a priority to eat and drink with outsiders? Rigid adherence to rules by the Pharisees makes them unwilling and unable to help those with deep needs, but Jesus demonstrates that he will jump over any obstacle to meet people who need to know that God loves them. How easy it is to exclude people who are different to us! Jesus saw beyond lifestyles and behaviour to the fact that all people have needs and questions. If you feel uncomfortable in the presence of unbelievers, remember why Jesus wasn't and ask God for more of his compassion.

Lord, help me to be sensitive to those I tend to look down on. Rather than judging them so quickly, help me to look at them with your eyes.

[1] Rom 5:8; 2 Thess 2:16,17

FASTING IS NOT THE ISSUE

Identify three life-giving characteristics of your relationship with the Lord. 'Lord, thank you that you have given me new life.'

Fasting was a common practice among the Jews. The annual Day of Atonement was the most important opportunity, but the Pharisees chose to fast two days of every week. Throughout the Old Testament, other times of fasting were called on special occasions when the help of God was needed. What surprises the Pharisees is that the disciples of Jesus do not appear to fast at all. Religious people may similarly criticise us when we step out of their boundaries and boxes. When his followers are accused of not fasting, Jesus defends them. When you are accused by others as a result of following the guidance of Jesus for you, expect no less; but remember, he's always right and you are right to follow his guidance.[1]

Jesus' response is interesting. He offers three pictures to enable his listeners to make an appropriate assessment of him and his authoritative answer (vs 16,17). He doesn't specifically respond to the question whether fasting is right or not. Instead, he provides them with an opportunity to decide if he has the authority to determine when fasting should occur. Matthew's implicit message is to declare that Jesus has the authority to determine how his followers should live. The questioners' problem was the fact that they were used to certain ways of practising fasting. Jesus offered an alternative - times of celebration balancing periods of fasting - and he encouraged them through his word pictures to follow it. The answers he offered to their question identified that his way was radical but beneficial; to follow their tradition would be to miss out on the potential of his new way. We too need to hear his challenge to ensure that our traditional ways of doing things enable rather than hinder the life and vitality his Spirit brings.

Lord, thank you that you have brought us into a relationship with you that is filled with life, hope and newness.

[1] Luke 6:46

JESUS IS IN CONTROL

Lord, help me to entrust to you the challenges in my life.

MATTHEW 9:18–26

The ages and problems of the women in these stories were different, but Jesus responds willingly to both. He treats them as individuals, ministering to them personally and differently. As women, they were both socially powerless, yet Jesus publicly exalts the woman who had had the haemorrhage because of her willingness to trust him, commending her and endorsing her healing. Similarly, in his resurrection of the girl he shows that not even death is an obstacle to the power of his love. In today's world, dominated by advertising and 'image', it's easy to believe that some people are more important than others. There is a danger that we may assume that God has favourites too. He doesn't. Every child of God is unique and therefore special. When you wonder if God is aware of your situation, remind yourself that he knows more about you than you know about yourself.[1] He's more concerned about you than you are yourself!

Matthew notes that the ruler asks Jesus to restore his daughter even though she has died. There is no indication in Matthew that Jesus has yet raised anyone from the dead, but the ruler believes that Jesus can do this. Why do we often fail to reflect the same confidence in Jesus as that expressed by the ruler? Similarly, the woman with the haemorrhage believed that a touch of Jesus' garment would be sufficient to bring healing. Both believed that Jesus could solve their impossible problems and both had their requests met. Meanwhile, we, as readers, have the opportunity to increase our appreciation of Jesus' unique authority. He is with us to touch us, whether we are aware of his presence or not. Ask the Lord to increase your faith.[2]

Lord, help me to realise that you are with me when I fear that I am on my own. Help me to recognise that my problems are opportunities to benefit from your support.

---

[1] Luke 12:6,7 [2] Luke 17:5

WILL PEOPLE NEVER LEARN?

Think of several examples of the Lord's kindness to you. Lord, thank you for your touch on my life in so many ways.

MATTHEW 9:27–34

These stories are not just recorded to establish Jesus' healing authority. They are also presented so that we may consider the appropriate response to those occasions when he touches our lives. Because of the readiness of the blind men to believe that Jesus could help them, he restored their sight. This was a remarkable miracle, especially since the Jews believed that to heal the blind was as difficult as raising the dead. Interestingly, there is no record of blindness being healed in the Old Testament, nor of anyone other than Jesus achieving this in the Gospels. Similarly, when the demoniac is brought to him, he dismisses the demon, resulting in the man being able to speak and the crowd being in awe. Matthew presents Jesus as being truly awe-inspiring. Take a moment to identify some things the Lord has done that leave you in awe of him.

In the light of these remarkable miracles and the supremacy of Jesus thus highlighted, the differing responses to him are significant. Some consider the evidence and come to an accurate decision concerning Jesus, but others do not. The blind men realise his true identity, while the sighted Pharisees claim he acts by the prince of demons (v 34). Even the blind men, however, have to learn that to confess Jesus must be followed by the appropriate response of obedience. Instead, the men disobey his command to keep silent; this probably made life more difficult for Jesus.[1] Moreover, the time for the disclosure of 'the Messianic secret' of who Jesus was had not yet come. He really does know better than we do! It is good to worship Jesus, but the sincerity of our worship is proved by our readiness to obey him.[2] Do you need to discipline yourself to obey the Lord in some way – to keep a confidence, for instance? Sometimes to keep quiet is harder than to speak!

Lord, may I never take you for granted. I acknowledge you as Lord and, on that basis, determine to obey you as fully as I can.

[1] *Compare* Mark 1:45 [2] 1 Sam 15:22; Luke 6:46; John 14:15

CALCULATION OR COMPASSION?

Pause a moment. Hold your nation before God. Ask him to show you it through Christ's eyes.

MATTHEW 9:35 – 10:4

Jesus' central message was the coming of God's reign. It was good news, embodied in himself, his teaching, preaching and healing (v 35). As he viewed his nation in the light of the kingdom, Jesus saw it to be hollow, lacking a centre. The people were prey to ungodly forces (harassed), unable to defend themselves (helpless), like 'sheep without a shepherd' (v 36). This was not a farming analogy, but an Old Testament image for Israel and the failure of its leaders.[1] The nation badly needed its true king. Many nations still experience the same combination of a poor, powerless and often oppressed majority with corrupt or inadequate leadership. In affluent nations a different hollowness applies: shallow consumerism, the undermining of the public good, and leaders lacking the moral vision necessary for effective change. Both are an offence to God's reign.

If we share Christ's perspective on our society, we are also called to share in his response, which was neither judgemental nor detached, but made out of deeply felt compassion. This divine compassion led to action, as he commissioned his disciples to share in his authority and take part in his ministry. They would not be sheep without a shepherd, for they would experience the great shepherd's care and share his ministry.[2] Only here, in Matthew, are the twelve called apostles (v 2). This is more than coincidental; the renewed Israel being formed is sent out to minister.

This harvest (v 37) is not the final judgement, but denotes the scale of the task of proclaiming the kingdom to the nation. Jesus shows compassion, not calculation of people's receptivity - an important reminder for us! Called first of all to prayer (v 38), the disciples find, as we do too, that they are made the answer to their own prayers.

How will you respond to Christ's compassionate call?

---

[1] Num 27:17; 1 Kings 22:17; 2 Chr 18:16; Zech 10:3 [2] John 10:27–29; 1 Pet 5:2–4

A MATTER OF JUDGEMENT

For what are you most grateful to God? What in your life shows your gratitude?

MATTHEW 10:5–15

Despite the urgency of the harvest it is, at this stage, restricted to Israel (vs 5,6). It was the same with Jesus himself.[1] Salvation history was being unfurled: first, Jesus' mission to Israel, and then, after his death and resurrection, the disciples' mission to 'all nations'.[2] Israel's election was for the blessing of others.[3] The same applies to renewed Israel. Matthew's primarily Jewish audience needed to know that God had remained faithful to his covenant promises.[4] Jewish believers had not become part of a different race or religion, but a renewed one. For now, the twelve share in this mission to Israel, but Matthew records it with the wider mission in mind. Their mission is parallel to their Lord's. They proclaim the message he shared with John the Baptist: 'The kingdom of heaven has come near' (v 7).[5] The healing activity is itself part of the proclamation of the kingdom. 'Has come near' means, 'touching you now', not 'will come as judgement soon'. Our lives and words are bearers of the kingdom.

The motivation for their mission, and for ours, is grace. Gratitude is the wellspring of all we do. We have received freely and are to give freely (v 8). The twelve can expect hospitality as they travel – not as payment for their ministry, but as the common ground they share with their culture. They are not to be self-sufficient. Mission is rarely one way: it assumes our common humanity, and creates new relationships.

'Peace' (shalom) was a customary greeting, a polite blessing they were to give, but true shalom (a word which sums up the breadth and depth of Israel's hope) only comes as a benefit of receiving the kingdom. Although the kingdom is 'near', the day of judgement remains on the horizon. The gravity of Christian mission is that to reject God's messengers can be to reject him also.

If, like Israel, we are called in Christ for the sake of others, what difference might this make in some practical way to how we live this week?

[1] Matt 15:24 [2] Matt 28:19 [3] Gen 12:1–3; Exod 19:5,6; Isa 42:6 [4] John 4:22 [5] Matt 3:2; 4:17

SHEEP, SNAKES AND DOVES

When have you felt most vulnerable? Consider how God has protected you in such situations, and thank him.

MATTHEW 10:16–23

The gospel is God's final word. It will either bring peace or division. There is no neutral territory. However disinterested people may appear, neutrality cannot be maintained. This divisive capacity, even within families, explains why Christian mission can meet such resistance, and Christian disciples such persecution.

Jesus gives instructions for the disciples' first mission trip, and takes the opportunity to warn them about the price they may have to pay. The potential scenario moves from welcome hospitality to persecution by families or the authorities. (Jesus himself will be brought before a council, a king and a governor, vs 17,18.) The future mission to the Gentiles is already implied here. Whether a society is intolerant of dissent or claims to be built on 'tolerance', the finality of the Christian message is often not seen as good news, and attempts are made to silence the messengers. The sheep metaphor is continued, to warn the missionaries of a hostile world where they will be vulnerable. They are to be discerning like snakes, while maintaining the innocence and integrity of doves (v 16).

Christians do not seek confrontation and are not to court persecution. However, if, out of faithfulness to our Master, we are brought before the authorities, the Holy Spirit will give us words to say (vs 19,20). Galilean peasants are being prepared to stand before kings for Christ's sake ('on my account', v 18). Those better educated need to rely equally on the Holy Spirit, rather than their own ability with words! Jesus calls his missionaries to constancy in discipleship (v 22). In verse 23, the coming of the Son of Man cannot refer to the second coming, but may refer to the fall of Jerusalem or to Jesus' resurrection and ascension, when he receives the kingdom from his Father.[1]

Christians don't always choose their battles well! What does it mean to be as shrewd as snakes in choosing when to make a public stand?

[1] Dan 7:13,14

FAITH AND FEAR

'The LORD is my light and my salvation – whom shall I fear?'[1]

MATTHEW 10:24–33

Christian faith requires open discipleship and public acknowledgement of Christ. Christians are to be publicly identified with their Lord, and people's view of the Lord will inevitably shape their view of us. However, a Christian's identity is grounded in one opinion alone: Christ's view of us, his willingness to acknowledge us before the Father (v 32).

Because our mission is an extension of Christ's, we can expect a similar response to the one he received. The threat of physical persecution may make us afraid, but there may be even greater pain in being accused of having false motives, or of being under the control of other demonic or psychological forces. The Pharisees had accused Jesus of this[2] and would do so again.[3] Those who proclaim the gospel of grace today can be accused of being on a personal power trip, simply because they bear witness to Christ's claims on all. One day God will ensure that all secret motives will be public information; for now, the gospel is not to be kept secret but 'proclaim[ed] from the roofs' (v 27).

Jesus intends his people to be tough enough to resist personal or religious insult (Beelzebub can be translated 'lord of the flies') or the threat of personal or psychological violence. They are not to give in to intimidation, because of their reverent fear of the Judge of all. This Judge they know as Jesus' Father, and they have been taught to address him as their Father (v 29; 6:6–18). The promise that they, and we, are worth more than many sparrows, is in one sense double-edged. The Father cares directly for even the seemingly most insignificant part of his creation – but sparrows do drop to the ground. Similarly, suffering for Christ frequently accompanies witness to Christ.

What is the difference between suffering for Christ and other suffering?

---

1 Ps 27:1   2 Matt 9:34   3 Matt 12:24

WHAT PRICE PEACE?

Search my heart, O God, and show me where my first love lies.

MATTHEW 10:34–42

These verses draw us to the heart of this section. The gospel of the kingdom is God's final word to humankind, and Jesus, the bearer of the kingdom, is the only one worthy of our absolute loyalty. His ministry did not develop by chance. 'I have come' (v 35) indicates clear intent. According to heaven's will, human life could not continue as it was, but had to be remade. Both Israel and, later, all nations would be divided between those who welcomed and those who resisted this heavenly remaking. The ultimate object of peace would only be reached through profound division, which could strike at the heart of family relationships, in a culture which honoured family highly. Jesus will not allow us to use our faith as an excuse to avoid our family responsibilities;[1] but he does require us to love him more. When Maria was considering whether or not to marry Hudson Taylor[2] she is alleged to have said, 'If he loves me more than he loves Jesus, he is not worthy of me.'

Jesus already had the cross in view. The remaking of the earth would cost more than division in a human family.[3] To follow Jesus is to take up the cross. This was not a metaphor in first-century Palestine, but meant 'losing your life'. Jesus' warning (vs 38,39) contrasts strongly with our culture's emphasis on self-actualisation.

Each disciple's cross is to be freely embraced, for Christ's sake. He is the ultimate source of our motivation. If the kingdom is anything like the King, it is worth more than everything else put together! It is this level of identification with Jesus, out of love for him, which makes us truly his representatives. Something implied throughout the chapter is made explicit here (v 42). We may be 'little ones', but to receive us is to receive him, and the Father too.

Consumer religion helps me 'realise my potential', Christian discipleship teaches me to lose my life to find it. How can I turn from self to Christ?

[1] John 19:26,27; 1 Tim 5:8 [2] Pioneer missionary to China, 1832–1905
[3] Matt 27:46

WHAT IF I'M WRONG?

Compassionate Lord, teach me to be honest when I doubt, yet always sure of your goodness.

MATTHEW 11:1–6

The problem with shouting the gospel from the rooftops is, what if we are wrong? John the Baptist last appeared in the Gospel when he was arrested (4:12). He had baptised Jesus, spoken of the one who would baptise with the Holy Spirit, and seen the Holy Spirit descend upon him.[1] John had suffered for his faithfulness, having made a public stand about his king's adultery.[2] His problem was not 'suffering' in itself, but whether he was suffering for nothing. He had believed Jesus was the Messiah, but now struggled with doubts. If Jesus was the Messiah, why was John still in Herod's prison? And why was there still a Herod?

John's confusion was understandable; he had two conflicting understandings of the kingdom. He stood at the transition between the present age and the breaking-in of the new.[3] John, like others in his day, expected the kingdom in its fullness, including judgement on the Gentiles, to be simultaneous with the coming of the Messiah. The axe was at the root of the tree and the fire about to fall.[4] His problem with Jesus' ministry was that too much was happening to ignore, but not enough to convince. John expected much more! But Jesus' teaching about the kingdom was that it was both 'already' and 'not yet'. It had invaded the old age without displacing it. For a time, good and evil would exist together. The final judgement had not yet come!

In the kingdom there are already things to 'hear' (chs 5-7) and to 'see' (chs 8,9). Jesus transforms lives now and promises a future. He asks John to revise his theology in the light of Scripture, using phrases from Isaiah's Messianic passages (v 5).[5] It is easy to 'take offence' over Jesus, because we expect too much - or too little!

Doubt is not necessarily sin. It can be a stepping stone to better understanding. How can we help ensure that our faith is intellectually honest?

[1] Matt 3:11–17 [2] Matt 14:3,4 [3] Matt 11:13 [4] Matt 3:10 [5] Isa 29:18,19; 35:5,6; 42:7; 61:1

JOHN THE HINGE

Jesus, my greatest treasure, help me to seek after whatever is great in your eyes.

MATTHEW 11:7–15

Despite John's doubts, Jesus does not undermine him but publicly honours him as the hinge upon which the kingdom turns. (Christ's view of us is not dependent on the accuracy of our theology.) John is honoured for his consistency and godly distinctiveness. He does not vacillate like Herod, whose coins bore the emblem of a swaying reed. The only king's palace John ever lived in (v 8) was the one in which he was imprisoned. He has faithfully fulfilled Scripture to the best of his understanding. (May the same be said of each of us!) He was the forerunner, preparing the way for the Lord's coming,[1] and the fulfilment of the promised return of Elijah.[2] John even dressed like Elijah![3] Jesus describes him as 'more than a prophet' (v 9), the greatest human being to live before Christ. Greatness is measured not by worldly success but by faithfulness to the purposes of God.

Accurate theology matters. Jesus' words in verse 11 do not lessen his tribute to his cousin. They do not compare people, but eras. There is no way to compare the kingdom of heaven, revealed in the coming of Jesus, with anything before it. Until Jesus came, the Hebrew Scriptures were a collection of stories begging for an ending. Jesus' statements about John show us how the two Testaments relate. Following Jesus' own use of Scripture, early Christians, including Matthew, interpreted it in the light of his coming. Hence the many quotations from it in this Gospel.

By talking about John like this, Jesus was talking, indirectly, about himself. He is the fulfilment of the Law and the prophets.[4] Verse 12 is difficult, with several possible interpretations. Does the kingdom advance vigorously, or is its advance violently resisted? As each Gospel progresses towards the cross, the latter is the most likely.

We cannot understand Jesus without knowing the Old Testament. Which parts do you know, and which do you need to get to know?

---

[1] Mal 3:1 [2] Mal 4:5 [3] Matt 3:4 [4] Matt 5:17

MY GENERATION?

Saviour of the world, teach me to know when I need to weep for my generation!

MATTHEW 11:16–24

Reviewing the response to his and John's ministry, Jesus sees his generation as marked by unbelief. It looked for reasons not to believe and found excuses not to disturb its way of life. John, despite his popularity,[1] seemed too ascetic and to be overemphasising judgement. Jesus, to whom crowds also flocked,[2] was seen as keeping bad company, his mercy extending too far. Like our Lord, we need to read our generation in the light of God's kingdom.

Jesus had committed himself to those seen as furthest from God. His meals shared with social and religious outcasts both portrayed the kingdom and put it into practice. A consistent part of his ministry,[3] this brought him criticism from those who thought they had no special need of God's mercy. A Christlike church will also be open to criticism for its consistent compassion to the undeserving.

Jesus was not making a sideswipe at his culture in general. Nor should we! Rather, he referred to specific communities. 'Woe to you' (v 21) expresses regret, not vengeance. He had lived in Capernaum and was grieving for the blindness of people he knew. His teaching and healing were meant to open the possibility of repentance, but could not guarantee it! His ministry increased the culpability of his unresponsive audience. It would be worse for these communities than for those involved in the pagan arrogance of Tyre and Sidon[4] or the moral and economic degeneration of Sodom.[5] If all are in need of repentance, the greatest sin is not the most flagrant, but the most arrogant.

Jesus' grief over his generation's blindness did not cause him to withdraw. He continued to teach, preach and heal. The apostles, three of whom came from Bethsaida, are commissioned with renewed urgency. Apparent disinterest is not to halt the church's mission.

What tempts you to give up? Not to give up believing but to give up public witness and active evangelism? What keeps you going?

[1] Matt 3:5; 14:5 [2] Matt 4:24,25 [3] Matt 9:10–13; 22:8–10 [4] Ezek 26–28
[5] Gen 18,19; Ezek 16

THE FATHER'S PLEASURE

Teach me, Father, to take pleasure in whatever pleases you, as Jesus did.

MATTHEW 11:25–30

These verses show why Jesus continues his mission, despite the indifference of the Galilean villages. He sees the Father at work in his ministry, so grief ('woe to you') and praise belong together. The words 'Father, Lord of heaven and earth' (v 25) reveal an intimate relationship with the Creator. Jesus' identity is not found in success or failure, but in his relationship with his Father.

Even in Jesus' incarnate life there is a mutual dependence. The Father hides and reveals, but cannot be known unless the Son reveals him. Here we see God's mission: salvation comes from the Father, through the Son in the power of the Holy Spirit.[1] Ultimately, the kingdom is not merely God's restoration of his creation but the knowledge of God himself. This is why present experience of the kingdom, however incomplete, is supremely more valuable than anything 'until John' (v 13).

Knowledge of the Father comes through revelation (God's 'gracious will'), not intellectual capacity. It is hidden from the wise, not because they cannot know it but because they cannot know it through wisdom. We believe in order to understand,[2] not vice versa. The Father and Son are at work, but those who like the world as it is cannot see. The Father's hiding and revealing is not arbitrary. It is a confirmation of choices already made.

Jesus' invitation comes to the weary and burdened (revisiting the 'harassed and helpless' of 9:36.) His yoke demands everything, but is light because it is borne with him, not just for him. It is easy because it is 'learning from' him and he 'is gentle and humble in heart'.[3] Those who invite others to come to him need the same qualities.

The Father has so designed our salvation that power and cleverness give no advantage. If this is so, how should it be reflected in our churches?

---

[1] Matt 3:16,17 [2] So Augustine of Hippo, 354–430, and Anselm of Canterbury, 1033–1109 [3] See also 2 Cor 10:1

LOVE AND TRUTH MEET

In the Lord's presence today, thank him for his grace which draws you to him and enables you to live in obedience.

MATTHEW 12:1–8

'Unfailing love and truth have met together.'[1] These words underline the tension of the two incidents with which Matthew begins this section of his Gospel. Jesus' critics thought that the truth of the Sabbath principle was far more important than an act of love. It is truth that the Sabbath is God-given and good for us. Its principle of rest is like the Creator enjoying the fruit of a week's labour.[2] Rest is also freedom from thinking we can achieve our own self-sufficiency – a lesson the Hebrews had to learn by being fed with manna in the desert.[3] We may need disciplines in our lives to help us keep resting in God, but rules that override the exercise of grace go too far.

Unfailing love is seen in Jesus' allowing his hungry disciples to gather corn to eat (v 1), as David provided for his men of old (vs 3,4), and giving priority to a crippled man (v 13). For the key principle is that Jesus himself is Lord of the Sabbath, and he himself brings together covenant mercy with covenant obedience. For the Jews, keeping the Sabbath, along with circumcision and sacrifice, was meant to be their covenant expression of gratitude and dependence on God. The problem arose when they thought that when they performed such acts, they no longer needed mercy.

As increasingly our children take responsibility for their own lives, we try to teach them by letting them see and feel the consequences of wrong choices. But, like the Pharisees, we can sometimes become hard and insensitive in the pursuit of very good principles. Jesus did not make truth cancel out covenant loyalty, but said that they needed to embrace to make a greater whole. When we need wisdom to balance truth and grace we must ask, 'What would the Lord of the Sabbath do?'

Jesus told a story of a wayward son receiving forgiving grace and a bitter elder son faithful to his family obligations.[4] Is there a place for both grace and faithfulness in your family and church relationships?

---

[1] Ps 85:10a, NLT [2] Gen 2:2,3 [3] Exod 16:15–26 [4] Luke 15:11–32

RIGHT AND WHOLE LIVING

Jesus invites us, 'Come to me ... and I will give you rest.'[1] Relax your body and soul as you come to him this day.

MATTHEW 12:9–14

Most translations include this passage under the same heading as verses 1–8. Again, we see those who were jealous of Jesus' power (they assumed he could heal!) looking for an opportunity to accuse him. Again, a legalistic and self-serving understanding of the obligation to keep the Sabbath overrides compassion. This time Jesus asserts his Sabbath Lordship by a miracle which enables the crippled man to return to full life (and perhaps a new possibility of employment and self-respect). But he also takes the opportunity to confront their wrong understanding of the value of every human being (v 12). Mark tells us[2] that Jesus was angry and deeply distressed by their attitude, which pitted religious stability against the man's need.

Right living (righteousness) and whole living (shalom) belong together, the psalmist reminds us.[3] A key reason for the Sabbath is our wholeness, so we cannot dismiss this controversy as of another era. Jesus is still Lord of the Sabbath, and demonstrates 'the grace of God which wills our wholeness'.[4] How we seek shalom in everyday life is a real issue for us. We dare not claim, however, that wholeness always depends on physical well-being. Our own experience tells us that healing does not always come via a miracle, though God's grace is always sufficient, even in weakness.[5] Grace is often manifest in the ordinary as much as in the spectacular for it is in the stresses of life that character is revealed and matured. Eugene Peterson's paraphrase of Paul's call to service makes this connection to the ordinary very clear: 'Take your everyday, ordinary life – your sleeping, eating, going-to-work, and walking-around life – and place it before God as an offering.'[6]

How can you share your healing with others who are also wounded? Do you have perseverance to support those for whom there is no physical healing this side of heaven?

[1] Matt 11:28 [2] Mark 3:5 [3] Ps 85:10b, *The Message* [4] Augsburger, 'Matthew', *The Preacher's Commentary*, Nelson, p145 [5] 2 Cor 12:9 [6] Rom 12:1, *The Message*

BRUISED REEDS NOT BROKEN

Recall friends who have encouraged you in the faith, and thank God for them.

MATTHEW 12:15–21

A pastor friend, influential in my early years of ministry, had a strident declamatory style of preaching of the kind not now in favour and a strong sense of mission energised by his pursuit of causes. But his heart was soft towards those who were struggling in life and he gave much time to their support. As I saw these people coming to his door, I often thought of them as his 'bruised reeds'. He enjoyed the inference that he was like his Master (v 20), at least in this.

In the context of the plotting between the religious and the secular authorities, Matthew uses a long quotation from Isaiah presenting the ideal picture of the expected Messiah.[1] Applied to Jesus, it emphasises that though he is on a powerful and world-changing mission, he is not recklessly fanning the opposition nor seeking unnecessary confrontation. Indeed, at this stage, he wants no publicity about his many miraculous healings. It is not yet time for the Messiah to be revealed, for he has much to do and much to teach his disciples.

When the time comes, there will be no doubting Jesus' steadfastness or determination, but along with this strength, he will also be able to accept weakness in others. This Messiah is the great encourager and restorer, as Peter and the other disciples who abandoned him on the night before his crucifixion discovered.[2] The art of leading people with vision and persistence is not always combined with patience at the foibles of lesser mortals. We are all familiar with the musical producer who drives the performers to get the best out of them and so becomes a perfectionist dictator. Such personalities are not unknown in churches which put great store on 'excellence for the kingdom' – but at what cost to a key kingdom value?

The task of the church has been described as disturbing the comfortable, and comforting the disturbed.[3] How well does your church follow Jesus' example in pursuing both of these tasks?

---

[1] Isa 42:1–4 [2] Luke 24:45–53; John 21:15–19 [3] William Temple, 1881–1944

THE STRONGER MAN

God's 'perfect love drives out fear.'[1] Ponder the promise of these words for us today.

MATTHEW 12:22–37

Can you imagine a demonised man set free by a miraculous deliverance in your church or Christian group? Most of us would witness such an event with many questions, perhaps not voiced, but uppermost in our mind. Is this real? Was the person in fact demonised? Or was it simply (but miraculously) recovery from a form of mental illness? Those examining Jesus' actions that day had no doubt the man was delivered from an evil spirit but their questions were of another kind. The people wondered about Jesus' identity (v 23). The Pharisees, on the other hand, wanted to know what his connection was with the prince of demons – 'Beelzebul' in contemporary slang. Was Jesus himself using, or possessed by, satanic power (v 24)? His answer makes it clear it was neither, and in so doing he gives further instruction on his own identity and his redeeming work through the Spirit.

The stern wording of verse 32 has sometimes caused anguish to those of tender conscience, but anyone who fears offending against God's Spirit cannot be included in this warning. Rather Jesus is calling 'blasphemy' any suggestion (as the Pharisees voice here) that God's work is being done through Satan, or that there is a power superior to his Holy Spirit. Those who ascribe God's work to Satan, failing to recognise his emancipating power, will not be forgiven. Neither is neutrality possible (v 30). Those who align themselves with God's Spirit are his and experience his freedom. If they let him, he continues to touch new areas of their lives and release them from all the things that bind them. 'Forgiveness is always in relationship … forgiveness cannot be known if one is closing his life to God.'[2]

What binds you today? A sin or a memory from the past? A fear for the future? Perhaps even a demonic influence? Surrender to the greater power of the Holy Spirit.

[1] 1 John 4:18 [2] Augsburger, 'Matthew', p150

ONLY THE HUMBLE REPENT

Selfishness has been called the curse of our age. Thank God for the cure he has made available to you in the cross.

MATTHEW 12:38–50

These critics of Jesus are never satisfied! An exorcism is not a sign? And if they had understood Jesus' reference to his own death and burial, that wouldn't have satisfied them either, because he is himself the sign. He is greater than Jonah and the Queen of Sheba, and his reign extends beyond the bounds of the nation and family. Jesus' diagnosis is that they are more firmly under the rule of the evil one than ever before, because the alternative – acknowledging God's reign – requires the humility of repenting of their adulterous allegiances.[1]

So Jesus tells a little story of an evil spirit, thrown out of a cleansed house, returning with seven housemates who prefer the comfort of a roof over their heads to the restless desert. It illustrates the desperate plight of his enemies under the sway of the evil one. But linking it with the picture of the 'stronger man' setting us free, it is a reminder that when our lives have been swept clean by the Holy Spirit new habits must replace the old, fresh spiritual disciplines reform our lives, and God's way of thinking supplant the old patterns of thought. A vacuum will be filled: if not by God's ways of living, then a person will revert to old patterns by default.

In many Western societies demonisation is becoming more common due to the rise of interest in the occult and various New Age practices. We need not be afraid of demons, for the Lord Jesus is greater than any evil power. But we do need to take seriously our responsibility to help those rescued from evil to live a Spirit-filled life.

Has God been leading you to help someone oppressed by evil forces? Ask the Lord for the Spirit's enabling to help them follow new paths of righteousness.

---

[1] Jer 3:6–11; Hos 3:1 – 4:1

GREAT EXPECTATIONS!

Praise you, Lord, for your great humility in freely offering salvation to all, though so many reject your good news.

MATTHEW 13:1–9

As Jesus moves his teaching from the synagogue to the seashore, Matthew records the first in a series of seven parables of the kingdom, beginning with one that occurs in all of the first three Gospels. It is typically used by preachers to challenge us to respond to the seed scattered by the master sower - a parable of the soils in which our hearts may have varying responses. To hear it afresh today, however, consider the soils to represent those friends and neighbours for whom you are praying. Can you identify some whose response is like a path - stamped down hard between the rows - exhibiting shut minds? Others may be rather stony - thin soil over limestone bedrock - shallow people not sustaining their interest. You may know others who are inclined to let the thistles of many distractions crowd the seedlings out. But there will also be fertile soil - hearts open to receive the 'word' of the gospel. Notice that, knowing the results will vary greatly, the sower still takes the risk of sowing. In the coming in of the kingdom of God we will live through failure, disappointment, loss - but also fruit. We can have confidence in the gospel to make a difference!

Was Jesus always successful in his lifetime? Some chose not to follow him. Some went back after beginning the journey. Most denied him and a few turned back again. Jesus tells the parable of the sower to warn us of varying responses and to encourage wholehearted obedience to his words (vs 9,23). He also encourages us to expect an eventual harvest, though it will not be uniform, as the seed may take time to germinate and early growth may be hidden for a while. Jesus knew what he was doing when he sowed undaunted, and he invites us to join him in his mission.

My word '... will not return to me empty, but will accomplish what I desire ...'[1] Are your expectations high as you pray and share Christ with your friends?

[1] Isa 55:11

WHY PARABLES?

Recall a time when a sudden insight taught you more about your Saviour. Treasure the added depth this gives to your relationship.

MATTHEW 13:10-17

'Why are you using parables?' Jesus' disciples asked, as he switched to this form of teaching (v 10). The first flush of publicity is fading and people are proving deaf to his call to discipleship, even as opposition is building among the power-brokers threatened by his public presence. Parables are a way of safely holding the attention of the crowds while preserving his teaching until they are ready to receive it.[1] Many will recall the story even if they don't yet have the key to understanding it.

Jesus has a deeper reason for his methodology, however: '... understanding depends upon the recognition of Jesus as the Messiah and upon the recognition of the kingdom of God which is breaking forth in his ministry.'[2] The parable is an instrument of revelation for those on the inside. Jesus' emphatic 'given to you' (v 11) and 'blessed are your eyes' (v 16) make a clear distinction between those in the inner circle and those still outside it. Not that he is implying some form of mystery cult or secret society - a spirituality common to Gnostic philosophy. Rather, he promises that commitment to him will bring with it increasing insight. The biblical 'secret' is always something revealed to people through him.[3] Of course, those who at one point are on the outside - like Jesus' family in 12:46,47 - can later change and become insiders.[4]

We know the power of an idea we discover ourselves. The insight of the 'aha!' experience stays with us long after didactic teaching has left us. In encounter with Jesus, there is enough light to convict and convince us to enter the kingdom, but real learning and spiritual growth occur after that entry.

We are part of the 'blessed' (v 16) - the happy company on the inside who see and hear what was not possible before Jesus came. Thank God for your growth in understanding.

---

[1] *Compare* Mark 4:33,34 [2] EC Hoskyns, *The Riddle of the New Testament*, quoted by RVG Tasker, *Matthew*, pp136,137 [3] Col 1:26,27; 2:2 [4] Acts 1:14

ARE YOU REALLY LISTENING?

**Give me a hearing heart, O Lord, that longs to understand your words
and to respond with wholehearted devotion.**

MATTHEW 13:18–23

Though the parable of the sower is one of the most elaborate of Jesus'
parables, and the one he explains in detail to his inner circle, we
must resist the temptation to turn it into allegory or try to interpret
every element. In considering verses 1–9 we applied the soil types
to our friends and noted that, though we can anticipate different
responses to the sowing of the Word, we can have confidence in the
final success of his kingdom.

Now, as we hear the parable again, we listen to it as a challenge
to ourselves personally. Jesus begins emphatically: 'Hear ye' (v 18,
AV) or in Knox's paraphrase: 'The parable of the sower is for your
hearing.' The central point is that for each soil type the sower and
the seed are the same, and only the soil differs. So which am I? Does
God's Word bounce off me because I am hard or indifferent? Or
are my roots shallow so that I am quickly put off by difficulties and
opposition? Is the message squeezed out by cares or activities in a
cluttered life? Or is my fruitfulness being maximised because I am
receptive to God's promptings? Though the increase is God's[1] and
the fruit-bearing the Spirit's work,[2] I am nevertheless called to be a
faithful disciple, truly listening to the Master.

We do well to be wary of a practice of faith that is all head, not
engaging the heart or producing a holy life, but understanding God
and his ways is important. 'Your mind matters,' to quote a significant
book title by John Stott. God wants us to understand what he is
doing and what he desires us to do. Listening will be different at
every stage of our life, keeping us challenged until we no longer see
through a glass darkly, but know fully, face to face.[3]

**What kind of soil are you providing for God's Word? Is there a need for
a more intent listening which will have a greater impact on your living
and serving?**

[1] John 15:1–8; 1 Cor 3:6 [2] Gal 5:22,23 [3] 1 Cor 13:12

GOD IS AT WORK

Do you have a burning question you wish to ask your Lord? Put it into words and lay it before him.

MATTHEW 13:24–35

Here three parables address three questions that are just as relevant today. First, why does evil exist? Jesus says in reply: God's kingdom is like what happens when weeds are contaminating a crop. You may not initially be able to tell good from bad, but the separation will come eventually. In the meantime, you must suspend condemnation, for judgement belongs to God. Note, however, that Jesus says the field is the world (v 38) and the parable is about the kingdom rather than the church, so this parable does not forbid all church discipline.[1]

Secondly, why does God's kingdom seem so insignificant? Jesus' answer to this is that the kingdom of heaven is like what happens when a very small seed grows into a great tree (vs 31,32) and gives shade to all. Birds coming to roost would suggest to his hearers that Gentiles were also included. This 'mustard seed conspiracy'[2] is the good news that the kingdom will grow and grow despite its slight beginnings.

Thirdly, why is the kingdom so hidden? The kingdom of heaven is like what happens when the smallest amount of yeast influences the whole loaf (v 33). History has consistently shown that small groups, such as the Clapham Sect supporting William Wilberforce, or the Christians meeting weekly in East Germany before the Berlin Wall came down, can have great effect. Being hidden at first is not necessarily a bad thing. What does this mean for us today? God's kingdom of love is growing at his command, though it may be underground and we cannot see it. And while we cannot make people acknowledge God, we can look for signs that he is unobtrusively at work, for we are assured that there are people 'on the hunt for God'.[3]

Where in your life and church have you seen 'mustard seed faith' at work – something small making a big impact? Praise God for it!

---

[1] Matt 18:15–18 [2] The title of a book by Tom Sine, now out of print
[3] Ps 22:26, *The Message*

A STORY FOR OUR TIMES

Praise God that as Judge of all he will be completely just and fair – so we can safely leave all judgement to him.

MATTHEW 13:36–43

You can't distinguish the darnel weed from genuine wheat till the heads are filled. By then it's too poisonous to mix with the grain, but separating it has to be left till the harvest. For this 'in-between time', Jesus seems to be advocating wholesale tolerance (vs 28–30) – a value of Western society which illogically tolerates all behaviours except intolerance! We are aware, however, that Jesus also advocates some absolutes. Jesus alone is 'the Son of Man' to whom 'authority, glory and sovereign power' have been given.[1] All future judgement has been committed to him.[2] There is thus an ambiguity as regards judgement, and, at Jesus' command, we need to live with it. John the Baptist spoke of Christ's winnowing fork and purifying fire.[3] Perhaps in remembering this, we will leave judging to him.

Two areas of modern life call for withholding judgement. Generational differences are always with us, but intolerance of another generation's foibles or preferences seems to be increasing: for example in worship styles and ways of 'doing church'. We need to beware of letting the strengths and the weaknesses of our own generation influence our judgement of others, especially their expressions of spirituality – which can enrich our lives too if we let them.

In the secular sphere, fear of terrorism is encouraging people to suspect those 'not like us', especially those of another religion. 'Stranger danger' easily replaces 'hospitality to strangers',[4] even for followers of the Master who was not afraid to touch the man with leprosy or engage with the Gentile. We need to hold fast to our belief in a day of reckoning, but leave the judging to God; to value the kingdom greatly, but not be naive about present opposition; and to let Jesus teach us how to follow his example in our treatment of others.

In what ways can overzealous judgement of the world and its evils sometimes harm our mission as believers?

[1] Dan 7:13,14 [2] John 5:22,23 [3] Matt 3:11,12 [4] Heb 13:2

TIDINGS OF GREAT JOY

What gives you greatest joy in your relationship with Jesus? Thank him for it.

MATTHEW 13:44–52

It's a perennial question: 'What of those who have never heard? Will they be saved?' My answer is always that judgement is God's alone,[1] but how much better off we are knowing Jesus! We should desire this joy for everyone. Two of these parables illustrate this joy of discovery. One analysis of the parables highlights the central idea that finding the kingdom is like hidden treasure uncovered accidentally, treasure so great that it is worth selling everything to secure it; or like the joy of finding a priceless pearl after rigorous searching (vs 44–46). The weeds (vs 36–43) and net (vs 47–50) parables complement each other in stressing that judging is God's work done only at the end times. Understanding their background helps us translate the stories to our own day. It was common, for example, for people to bury treasure in jars when they feared invasion. Forgotten or abandoned, it could be found by a tenant farmer. My husband has an Italian colleague whose university office is crowded with ancient jars dug up and presented to him by his agricultural students. And while today we may worry over the ethics of it, Jewish law allowed the finder to keep the treasure: 'If a man finds scattered money, it belongs to the finder.'[2]

Likewise, the injunction not to judge another can be better understood when we appreciate how great was the trauma in the early church caused by Judas' defection.[3] That someone so close could betray his Master resonates with Paul's warning: '… if you think you are standing firm, be careful that you don't fall!'[4] Whether we connect with these stories in first-century dress or retell them in a contemporary context, we need to grasp both the joy of discovering Jesus and his call to commitment. Then we will be realising his concluding words - kingdom teaching has treasures both new and old (v 52).

'When we come to Christ we do not forget all the old in our lives but the new re-interprets the old.'[5] How has this worked in your experience?

[1] Gen 18:25; 1 Cor 4:5 [2] Michael Green, *Matthew*, BST; IVP, 2000, pp159,160 [3] Green, *Matthew*, p161 [4] 1 Cor 10:12 [5] Augsburger, 'Matthew', p170

HOME TOWN REJECTION

Praise God for the privilege of calling him Father.

MATTHEW 13:53–58

We skipped over a previous vignette regarding Jesus' mother and brothers (12:46-50), and now at the end of this section we get another glimpse of the familial setting of Jesus' ministry. If his mission prompted misunderstanding by his family and rejection by his home town, only those who have suffered similarly for the sake of the gospel can fully appreciate the cost involved. Barclay calls this 'one of the great human tragedies of Jesus' life'.[1] It is significant that Mary, who heard at the outset that a sword would pierce her soul,[2] was drawn to the foot of his cross,[3] for it is supremely the symbol of commitment taking precedence over all else. Both for Jesus and for Mary, accepting God's will above family considerations was very painful.

Today, however, we struggle with sacrifice of family life for the sake of mission. We question the choice made by pioneering missionaries to leave their families behind for years at a time. Indeed, the Christian church has sometimes so elevated the family that it is used to justify less than wholehearted service. Some have to renounce marriage 'because of the kingdom of heaven',[4] Jesus said, indicating that what may be asked goes beyond normal expectations of a stable family life.

True, there are physical as well as spiritual compensations. Jesus promises that no one who has left behind family or houses will be the poorer in the longer perspective.[5] Moreover, Jesus' followers are part of a new family. Human families often fall well short of the ideal. In fact, they can be destructive and dangerous places in our societies. But many people from dysfunctional or damaging families have found that the fellowship of the church, with the healing ministry of the Holy Spirit, has enabled them to experience a little more of what the Creator intends for family life.

Jesus' home town critics rejected his teaching and his miracles. How open are you to his wisdom and his healing in your family situation?

[1] W Barclay, *Matthew*, Vol 2, DSB; St Andrew Press, 1975, p52 [2] Luke 2:35
[3] John 19:25–27 [4] Matt 19:12 [5] Matt 19:29

REVENGE, FEAR AND EVIL

Lord, keep my heart so focused on you that I can hear your rebuke and not run from repentance.

MATTHEW 14:1–12

Moral and spiritual corruption in high places always has terrible consequences. In this case it results in the death of a good and innocent man. The combination of a woman bent on vengeance because her guilt has been exposed, and a blustering king captivated by an erotic dancer produces an act of appalling injustice. In fact there are so many things that contribute to the wrong: the imprisoning of John in the first place – which happens because he speaks unacceptable truth; then there is the folly of reckless promises, the fear of losing face before guests, and the ruthless conspiracy of mother and daughter who exploit the situation for the mother's own ends. Little can be more barbaric than the image of the head of a prophet served up at a birthday dinner on a plate.

Inevitably, in situations like this it is the God-fearing who suffer. John the Baptist was an early martyr for the faith, and there have been many more. In regime after regime, those who have exposed the evil around them in order to stay faithful to God have paid the price with their own lives; Christians who have refused to deny the truth have had power wielded against them. The same is true today. To refuse to compromise is costly in any circumstance, but against those who have the power to kill it may well carry the ultimate price.

We should not think of this passage, however, as merely about the actions of evil people. It shows us the seduction of sin in anyone's life when it works with weaknesses of character. Image-conscious Herod thought his rash promises made him look good – but they made him vulnerable and drew him into evil. We each need to recognise the flaws in our own characters and seek God's protection and victory over these weaknesses.

List those areas of your life where you feel most exposed to temptation, and bring them to God now.

GRIEF AND COMPASSION

'We have this treasure in jars of clay to show that this all-surpassing power is from God and not from us.'[1]

MATTHEW 14:13–21

It was many years before I understood that the context for the feeding of the five thousand was a profound bereavement. Having heard the dreadful news that his cousin had been beheaded, Jesus must have wanted nothing more than to be alone. Whenever we lose someone we love, even in normal circumstances, our feelings can be intense, our emotions taut. The fact that even Jesus needed to withdraw in sorrow (v 13) should help us to give more space to human grief. We may need time to experience its depth rather than rush away from it.

But Jesus' period of solitude was short-lived, for the crowds had other ideas and followed him. It is significant that even deep personal grief did not make him oblivious to the needs of others, or the desire to serve them. Jesus saw the crowd and had compassion on them. The sick were healed (v 14), the people taught.[2] He even cared about their ordinary bodily needs, and did not want them to go hungry. The amazing miracle where Jesus feeds the five thousand demonstrates that God cares about every aspect of our human lives. Satisfying hunger is as important to him as teaching people to pray.

Jesus' ministry is holistic. It cares for the whole person. And this should be the pattern for us today. We cannot split off evangelism from social action or counselling for they are all part of a whole. Here Jesus serves people in their emotional lives, their physical requirements, their mental understanding and their spiritual needs. And we must do the same. We may not be able to perform the same miracles for people, but we can share the same love. We can also provide resources that others can draw on in more needy lands for our joint ministry of care and compassion.

Write down all the incidents you can remember in the Gospels where Jesus addresses people's bodily needs.

---

[1] 2 Cor 4:7 [2] Mark 6:34

AUTHORITY AND FAITH

When our focus is fear, not faith, then it's not surprising that we fail. Lord Jesus, help me to fix my eyes on you today.

MATTHEW 14:22–36

The passage shows so many swings from fear to faith and back again. There is fear over the weather: sailing against sharp wind on a rough sea brings anxiety; it is hard work to stay afloat. Then there's sheer terror at the sight of a figure walking on water: surely no human can do that? Then they realise it's Jesus and fear gives way to faith; Peter feels he can walk on water too. But when he moves his gaze from Jesus to the rough sea, faith goes again, fear returns, and Peter begins to sink. It is only when Jesus climbs into the boat with him that his presence stills the storm and the disciples' faith is fully restored, and they worship Jesus as the Son of God.

Within a few hours, fear goes completely and faith takes over. For when the boating party draws into the shore they are surrounded by crowds of people who believe. Faith has become infectious, and people are brought to Jesus for healing. So great is the faith in the crowd that people only need to touch Christ's clothing to be healed. And the same Jesus who can stop the winds and waves – the natural forces of the creation – also stops the debilitating power of sickness and restores health.

Many of us experience both fear and faith in our Christian lives, and often close together. We can find deep assurance in prayer, only to have that dashed when we look at the circumstances around us and feel overwhelmed by the difficulties we face. So it is reassuring to know that God understands this and urges us to keep focused on Christ, even in our most terrifying circumstances. For Jesus is always with us and when he says 'You of little faith' (v 31) he is not condemning us but reminding us of his presence and encouraging us to greater trust.

What is your greatest fear? Bring that before God now, and ask him to give you the faith to overcome it.

LIP SERVICE IS NOT ENOUGH

Dear Father, what we say with our lips may we believe with our hearts and practise in our lives.

MATTHEW 15:1–9

The tendency to legalism lies very deep in the human psyche. And it almost always goes along with self-righteousness. Those here who are criticising Jesus' disciples would never dream of eating food without going through all the prescribed ritual washing. So they feel on safe ground when they remind Jesus of what the law requires. But they are not on safe ground, for Jesus knows all the deceit in their hearts. He knows that they are quite willing to distort God's commands, even bringing hardship to the elderly, when it suits them. In encouraging people to deprive parents of financial help, by declaring that such money is set aside for God, they are dishonouring God far more than if they ate with unwashed hands. They are colluding in injustice. In judging others they are under greater judgement themselves.

Jesus' quote from Isaiah reminds us of the difference between lip service and 'heart service'. Words on their own are hollow and futile, unless they are backed up with real heart commitment to God. Laws are empty unless their aim is to help us serve God better. In fact they can cause harm, create attitudes of smug self-satisfaction which keep us from God, and put barriers in the way of accepting one another.

The dangers of legalism are as real for us today as they were for the Pharisees and teachers of the law. How many people are turned off from church today by the attitudes of people who gather for worship? How often do Christians appear harsh and critical rather than loving and compassionate? And how often do we excuse our own faults whilst condemning similar failings in other people? A church that knows it has nothing to boast of is one that has been touched and released by God's Spirit. It is there that we'll see heart commitment rather than lip service, and love rather than judgement of others.

Have you criticised anyone recently or felt under judgement by another? If so, reflect on why this has happened and ask for God's release.

CLEANING UP THE HEART

'Search me, God, and know my heart; test me and know my anxious thoughts. See if there is any offensive way in me, and lead me in the way everlasting.'[1]

MATTHEW 15:10–20

Jesus does not worry that the Pharisees are irritated by him. He sees them as so lacking in vision that they are destructive leaders, but he does want to let the crowd know why he is not obsessed, like them, by the ablution laws. His approach to what makes people clean or unclean is different. The Pharisees' ritual observances focus on what and how people should eat, but Jesus says it is what comes out of the mouth, rather than what goes into it, that makes us 'unclean' (v 11). What we say reveals what we are like inside. So it isn't the dirt on our hands but the dirt in our hearts that we need to be worried about.

In his focus on the heart, Jesus taps into one of the Bible's deepest concepts. For the Bible talks of the heart as the 'religious concentration point' of our lives. It is where we respond to God, where we make all our key decisions, where we listen to the Holy Spirit, where we commit our lives. In Psalm 14, the fool says in his heart, not in his intellect, that there is no God. Jeremiah, the prophet, bewails the people's rebellious hearts[2] and tells us that the law is written on people's hearts.[3] Proverbs 10:8 reminds us that the wise in heart receive God's commandments, and Zechariah asks us not to hold evil in our hearts.[4]

The heart, then, is where we make our choices: where our hearts are, there our treasure is. But they are also where we harbour evil. And here the contrast between hands that can be washed clean and hearts where wickedness lodges is profound. Water is inadequate to clean away evil thoughts, adultery, hatred and lies. For these we need repentance and confession, and, most of all, the blood of Christ.

Reflect on this: Jesus invites us not to let our hearts be troubled or afraid,[5] and John assures us that even if our hearts condemn us God is greater than our hearts.[6]

---

[1] Ps 139:23,24 [2] Jer 5:23 [3] Jer 31:33 [4] Zech 7:10, NIV [5] John 14:1,27
[6] 1 John 3:18–20

A PERSISTENT PETITIONER

Lord, teach me how to pray with boldness and persistence, yet be ready to receive your reply whatever it is.

MATTHEW 15:21–28

The disciples are clearly annoyed at the pushiness and persistence of the Canaanite woman. As a non-Jew she did not have to observe all the protocols that Jewish people accepted, and she was making herself a nuisance. Even Jesus seems initially reluctant to get involved, but he will not simply send her away as they ask. Instead, he explains his ministry and calling to her – a courtesy not required by normal Jewish-Canaanite or male–female relations. He has come to minister to Jews alone: to take on the needs of every ethnic group would be to spread the resources far too thinly.

The woman has only one thing on her mind – her sick daughter. She has no doubt that Jesus can heal her. She doesn't argue against the unfairness of exclusion. She doesn't insist on moral rights or on what she deserves. She just begs. It is her very acceptance of her unequal status which seems to win the day. She is not asking to sit at the table and enjoy the rich food provided for the Jews. She just wants the crumbs that fall. And Jesus seems delighted with her reply. He commends her depth of faith and grants her petition.

What was it about this encounter that was so striking to Jesus? The woman's bold persistence? Probably. Her lack of intimidation? Possibly. Her faith? Definitely. But it was also her defenceless humility. She comes to him in her utter need, as the only one who can help. But she comes also in utter modesty, assuming nothing, ready to receive anything at all from Jesus. And surely that is true for us too. It is when we come humbly but boldly, with open hands to receive whatever God gives, that God can work the greatest miracles in our lives.

Are we content with whatever God blesses us with, or do we envy those who seem to have everything? Let us learn from the Canaanite woman.

FED AND SENT AWAY

Let us think of those who need food, those who need shelter, those who need a Saviour, and bring them to God.

MATTHEW 15:29–39

People had been following Jesus around, knowing he was God's chosen one. They were needy people. As with acute poverty today, their needs were basic. Healing was high on the list: body, feet, voice, sight. And Jesus loved them and met their needs with great healing miracles. They followed Jesus avidly for three days, even when they were physically drained. Out in the Galilean hills they were now hungry, cut off from food, and Jesus again met their need; from the most basic supplies he miraculously fed four thousand people.

Part of their attachment to Jesus, however, was out of hope of a deliverer, not least from Herod Antipas. A crowd that size would have been in danger if any of Herod's soldiers came across them, so Jesus had to disperse them safely. He did this, sending the crowd away (v 39). We tend not to think how odd this was. Thousands of people had gathered to hear this man and he was receiving gratitude and praise, but he sent them away. He was the shepherd and they were like sheep without a shepherd but he still sent them away. They may have been upset by this; they had given loyalty and followed him over long distances. But Jesus was not going to lead them on these terms. He dismissed them and went by boat to the area of Galilee thick with Herod's soldiers, Magadan near Tiberius, Herod Antipas' capital.

He did this for the people's good. The kind of national deliverance they wanted would not work; it would lead to death and bloodshed. It was important, even for these needy people, that they did not have Jesus on their terms. Being fed was not enough; and removing the yoke of Herod was not enough from Jesus' viewpoint. Nothing less than an open relationship with God as Father was on offer, and Peter would soon stumble towards that realisation.

Are there ways in which we want Jesus on our terms, even to the extent that he has to go away when we have been healed?

BE ON GUARD

O Lord, help me to assess my priorities and values honestly in the light of your teaching and example.

MATTHEW 16:1–12

Despite bitter theological feuding, the Pharisees and Sadducees were united in their unholy and passionate hostility towards Jesus. They were so profoundly threatened by him and so resistant to his message and character that they refused to recognise the evidence of God's power working through him. They weren't at all interested in 'a sign from heaven' (v 1) – they simply wanted to trip Jesus up.

Jesus warned his disciples to be vigilant in avoiding becoming like the Pharisees and Sadducees. Such attitudes as theirs are appallingly destructive of the spirituality and values that Jesus longs to see exhibited in any community of his followers. What's more, such preoccupations easily become ours, unless we are on our guard. There is tragic evidence of the influence of this particular virus in our churches today. Consider the symptoms displayed. They demonstrated an obsession with their own importance, expressed in the careful exhibition of religious qualifications and superiority. The Sadducees, a wealthy priestly elite, shared the Pharisees' love of wealth and status, while the Pharisees were obsessed with the externalities of religious ritual and the minutiae of religious law. There are striking parallels between these men and the leaders confronted by the prophets. Indeed, Jesus used the words of Isaiah and Hosea in his awful condemnation of the Pharisees.[1] How important it is for us always to remember the unbridgeable gulf between the attitudes personified by the Pharisees and Sadducees, and God's requirements: justice, mercy and humility.[2]

Finally, note the disciples' slowness to come to grips with the reality of Jesus' power. Occasions like this filled them with a longing 'to know Christ and the power of his resurrection …',[3] words Paul wrote while reflecting on the irrelevance of his Pharisaic qualifications.

Lord, protect me from foolish ambition and pride, and remind me of what is important to you.

[1] Isa 29:13 in Matt 15:8,9; Hos 6:6 in Matt 9:13; 12:7 [2] Mic 6:8 [3] Phil 3:10

WHO DO YOU SAY I AM?

Lord Jesus, may my acknowledgement of you as Christ impact greatly the way I live, and how I relate to the people around me.

MATTHEW 16:13–23

One minute Peter gets it completely right: understanding that Jesus is the Messiah. The next minute, he gets it completely wrong, failing to understand what Jesus must endure in order to fulfil his Messianic role. Peter, who was to become the acknowledged leader of the infant church, was capable of completely misunderstanding Jesus. It's noteworthy that the writer of the Gospel decided not to hide this. The story enhances the historical authenticity of the account, for there is no effort to protect the reputation of an important church leader.

Peter's acknowledgement of Christ's uniqueness occurred in a region of religious diversity, littered with the temples of various pagan gods, including one to Caesar. Surrounded by all this imposing religious architecture, the simply dressed religious teacher and his small band of followers, all of them from one of the empire's more marginal communities, would not have looked impressive. Yet it was here that Peter boldly expressed the conviction that was to shape the rest of his life, and eventually lead to his own crucifixion: 'You are the Messiah' (v 16). The church has often struggled to affirm the truth of these words with humility, and there are some who remain outside Christ's company and ignorant of his love because they struggle with his claim of unique status and authority.

Given this, how essential it is for us, as Jesus' representatives, to demonstrate the quality of his love, and not just talk about it. Words offer necessary explanations, but persistent actions of love lend integrity and authenticity to the words. This is why Paul urged disciples of Christ to imitate his love.[1] It is certainly critical today, given the increasing religious diversity and conflict in many societies and, at the same time, a growing intolerance of strongly held religious beliefs.

You, O Lord, are the Christ. Help me to serve you with humility and grace. Show me what this might mean practically this coming day.

[1] Eph 5:1,2

THE COST OF DISCIPLESHIP

Father, deepen my understanding this day of what it means for me to follow Jesus.

MATTHEW 16:24–28

Jesus never made it easy for his disciples to follow him. Not once did he try to 'sweet-talk' them into signing up – offering them all the privileges of membership, as it were, without indicating that the cost would be enormous. Evangelism that does otherwise is worse than negligent: it is irresponsible. In essence, Jesus required of his disciples exactly what was required of him, self-denial and a willingness to embrace rejection and suffering. No shallow triumphalism here! Each and every day we must strive to bring our minds and hearts into alignment with his. The rich young man's unwillingness to enter into such a commitment prevented him from experiencing the joy of Jesus' company, and also denied many poor people the opportunity for a better life.[1] Zacchaeus decided very differently, and brought great blessing to himself and others.[2] Our willingness to pay the cost of following Jesus has implications well beyond the personal. In every generation since Christ there have been women and men willing to turn their backs on earthly security, to risk ridicule and rejection, and in some cases even their lives, to demonstrate and proclaim the good news of Christ.

An Ethiopian colleague of mine abandoned a secure and well-paid position in an American university and returned to a war-torn country to look after destitute orphans. Why? Because years earlier when deciding to follow Christ he prayed, 'What is the service you have for me to do?' He could respond when the answer came because his trust was in Jesus, not in his bank account or job.

'... I beg you ... as an act of intelligent worship, to give him your bodies, as a living sacrifice ... let God re-make you so that your whole attitude of mind is changed ...'[3]

---

[1] Matt 19:20–23 [2] Luke 19:8–10 [3] Rom 12:1,2, JB Phillips' translation

SACRED SPACES

'Breathe on me, Breath of God; fill me with life anew.'[1]

What an extraordinary 'mountain-top' experience the three disciples had. It began in awe, moved to terror, and culminated in the peaceful embrace of Jesus. Then, when it was over, Jesus led them back down the mountainside. We are not told why these particular men were chosen to be witnesses to the transfiguration, and any guesswork on this matter is not particularly helpful. But Peter was absolutely right: it was good for them to be there, for they were direct witnesses of the Father's care for his Son. Jesus' motivation for retreating to the mountain top was to create space to pray.[2] Filled with dread at what lay ahead, he needed reassurance from his Father, which is exactly what he received. Immediately afterwards he offered his own reassurance to the terrified disciples (vs 6,7).

We also crave and need intimacy with God. Periods of quiet contemplation in which we deliberately set aside the space for conversation with God are essential. Many activists find this a real challenge, but it is one we must meet. However, there is another sacred space we need to inhabit if we are to remain close to Jesus. We must follow him back down the mountainside, back down into the midst of suffering humanity. Jesus was drawn, inexorably, to people in pain, just as they were drawn to him. Whatever the cause of their suffering and pain: physical or mental illness, social alienation by neglect or persecution, spiritual oppression or confusion, Jesus came to them, offering healing and peace, restoring dignity and hope. This is where we will find Jesus, and this is where he wants us to be.[3]

Have you achieved a healthy equilibrium between your inward and outward journeys? Prayerfully consider this question, and if necessary make it a matter for continued prayer.

---

[1] Edwin Hatch, 1835–89 [2] Luke 9:28,29 [3] Matt 25:34–36

IMPOTENT FAITH

Faithful God, help me to walk the pathway of faith.

MATTHEW 17:14–21

Jesus immersed himself in the realities of human pain, and no person who sought his restorative touch went away disappointed. In this case, a father's anguish at his son's terrible suffering led him to Jesus and his disciples. The disciples failed to make a difference, which is possibly the main reason for the inclusion of this story in the Gospel account, but Jesus cured the boy. Who of us cannot identify with the disciples' impotence and the inadequacy of their faith? Today there are clearly many people who are captivated by what they know of Jesus, but alienated by the church. Wise people are still seeking Jesus, but often they are not attracted to look for him in our company, the fellowship of Jesus' followers. They may not have good reason for this, but too often they do! Given all this, it is important for us to respond as the disciples did, not with defensive self-justification but with prayerful enquiry. The former leads us into the spiritual desert of the Pharisees and Sadducees, but the latter leads to a richer encounter with Christ. The disciples' greatest qualification was their dependency upon Jesus, and their sincere desire to know him more fully. This made possible the tiny faith that taps into the power of God.

I have been deeply affected by my encounter with a rural Nepali family in May 2005. Their direct experiences of God's healing power led them to a joyfully committed discipleship in a community that was very hostile towards Christians. In a context where there is no state welfare, their conversion severed them from the only external support they had, the goodwill of their neighbours. This has now dramatically changed, thanks to the quality of their lives, and a new church of more than fifty people has grown up around them. Peter was right![1]

'Faith is, for Jesus, not a matter of intellectual assent, but of practical reliance on a living God.'[2] Prayerfully reflect on this truth.

[1] See 1 Pet 2:11,12 [2] RT France, *Matthew*, TNTC; IVP, 1985, p266

WHAT REALLY COUNTS?

'This is how we know what love is: Jesus Christ laid down his life for us ...'[1]

MATTHEW 17:22–27

For a second time Jesus forewarns the disciples of his death, and for a second time he tells them that he will be raised back to life after three days. But this time the reaction is very different. It seems that at least part of Jesus' message is beginning to sink in – that he is going to be betrayed and killed – and the disciples are consumed with grief. Their lives had been so enriched by his presence and love that the prospect of his being violently wrenched away filled them with dread. The promise of his resurrection, it seems, remained utterly beyond their comprehension. It was only as they gazed with astonished eyes upon his resurrected body that they could truly begin to understand all that he had taught and done, in particular the staggering and wonderful implications of his action on the cross.[2]

The discussion prompted by the temple tax was trivial by comparison. Despite the fact that rabbis were exempt from the tax, and the knowledge that his true status provided him with even greater grounds for exemption, Jesus was prepared to pay it. Rather than cause unnecessary offence, he believed it was better to contribute the two drachma, about two days' pay for an average worker, and avoid being embroiled in trivial debate. He could leave that to the Sadducees, whose opposition to the temple tax was well known. There is a lesson here for us. We have been given the immense responsibility of continuing Jesus' mission in the world.[3] There is so much still to be done, both in sharing the truth of the gospel and in living out the implications of the good news of God's love and justice. What a tragedy it is, therefore, that we allow controversies of a lesser nature to bedevil our churches, distracting us from these essential responsibilities, and sapping our energy and resources.

Pray for your church leaders to have the wisdom to concentrate energy and resources on the continuation of Jesus' mission in the world.

[1] 1 John 3:16 [2] *See* Luke 24 [3] John 20:21

MISGUIDED PREOCCUPATIONS

Lord, we so often think and act wrongly, help us to get it right.

MATTHEW 18:1–14

Jesus' heart must have sunk a little when he heard the disciples' question. There was still so much they failed to understand about his kingdom and its values. An obsessive preoccupation with status is present in every human society, and it easily contaminates the church. We need to exercise great vigilance about the world's influence on our thinking and behaviour. Jesus was creating a very different society out of his followers. This new society was to be 'the living embodiment of the gospel, a sign of the kingdom of God, a demonstration of what human community looks like when it comes under his gracious rule'.[1] Jesus used their question as an opportunity to remind them that it is the 'poor in spirit' who will make up the kingdom of heaven,[2] and proceeded to teach them about relationships in this new community. In Jewish society a young child was 'one to be looked after, not looked up to'.[3] A young child had no status or authority, but was utterly dependent upon their parents.

Only when we recognise our total childlike dependence upon God can we enter God's kingdom. It's that same recognition, that same humility, which releases us to participate fully in the work of the kingdom. It's impossible to exaggerate the profoundly radical implications of Jesus' teaching about status and hierarchy, and how utterly subversive it is. A wonderful example can be seen in Paul's truly astonishing plea to a Christian slave owner to welcome back a runaway slave, a status-less piece of property, as a 'person and as a fellow believer in the Lord'.[4] How important it is to have particular regard for the people of low or no status in our society, and to be freed from hankering after status ourselves.

Ask God to help you identify and deal with your own vulnerabilities regarding preoccupation with status and hierarchy. How might this change the way you relate to others in your church and community?

[1] John Stott, *The Contemporary Christian*, IVP, 1992, p253 [2] Matt 5:3 [3] France, *Matthew*, p270 [4] See Phlm 16

HEALING RELATIONSHIPS

Have you ever had a serious disagreement with a fellow Christian? How did you resolve it?

MATTHEW 18:15–20

This is a straightforward piece of practical, pastoral advice relating to church discipline. Misunderstandings can best be resolved face to face rather than by letter or email. If that can be done privately, so much the better, but if not, then witnesses are necessary to establish truth objectively. It is amazing how our personal bias makes us selectively deaf. Discipline involving the whole church is extremely rare in Western churches, if it happens at all, but Matthew is quite clear that the good name of the Christian community may require it, though only after the most careful evaluation of the facts.

But it is Matthew's reference to the excluded member being treated as a 'tax gatherer' that is most surprising. Is Jesus adopting the anathematising practices of Judaism? Some commentators believe so, but that cannot be right. Matthew, above all people, could only make this reference to his old job if he saw the possibility that the offending brother would eventually be restored to church fellowship. If it was necessary to excommunicate, that need not be the final solution. Indeed, the whole purpose of discipline is to restore, as Paul made clear.[1]

The final verses of this section emphasise the central role of prayer, specifically in matters of church discipline but also in the widest context. The promises are so all-embracing that it is hard to take them literally. Does God really take such notice of our prayers when we are united in trustful dependence on him? 'Those who trust him wholly find him wholly true.'[2] Like similar promises elsewhere,[3] they relate to things which glorify God rather than ourselves, fulfilling his purposes and not our own.

How does your church deal with internal conflict? Does this passage offer any help?

[1] 1 Cor 5:5 [2] FR Havergal, 1836–79, *Like a River Glorious* [3] John 14:12–14

SHARING FORGIVENESS

You can't have one without the other.

MATTHEW 18:21–35

Peter's suggestion of a seven-fold forgiveness was remarkably generous. Rabbinic teaching suggested that God forgives three times but punishes on the fourth offence, based on Amos, chapters 1 and 2.[1] But Jesus gives a totally different insight into the heart of God.

It is always difficult to give current equivalents to the currency of Jesus' time but the ratio between the debts of the two servants was approximately half a million to one. The annual revenue of the province of Galilee was 300 talents so a debt of 10,000 talents was more than a king's ransom. Jesus takes the argument to extremes to make his point.

The problem, as with most of Jesus' teaching, is in actually doing it. A dear friend of mine holds back from becoming a Christian because he finds it impossible to forgive someone who offends him. He rightly takes with the utmost seriousness what Jesus is saying. We cannot enjoy God's forgiveness without sharing it. Freely we have received so we have to give with equal generosity,[2] yet who could calculate the number of churches which are crippled by unresolved grudges and the festering wounds caused by the unwillingness to forgive?

The Jesus whose dying prayer was for the forgiveness of his murderers[3] is also the Jesus who speaks the final words of the passage. If we will not receive and give away God's forgiveness then we will feel the direct outworking of his holy hatred of sin.[4] We cannot be forgiven without passing it on.

'"I can forgive but I cannot forget," is just another way of saying "I cannot forgive".'[5]

---

[1] Amos 1:3,6,9,11,13; 2:1,4,6 [2] Matt 10:8b [3] Luie 23:34 [4] Matt 6:14,15
[5] Henry Ward Beecher, 1813–1887

HARDENED HEARTS

'We are the people of his pasture, the flock under his care. Today, if you hear his voice, do not harden your hearts ...'[1]

MATTHEW 19:1–15

The Pharisees reappear with a hot potato of current debate – what are valid grounds for divorce? Opinions varied, but if Jesus is really a teacher, he should have his own interpretation. It is a sprung trap (v 3). In answering, Jesus characteristically probes beneath the presenting issue to the heart of the problem. The divorce legislation of Deuteronomy 24:1-4 must be interpreted by earlier revelation. Jesus grounds his ethic in the Creator's original purpose, revealed in Genesis 1:27 and 2:24, to create a deep unity between husband and wife, at every level of their beings – 'one flesh' (v 5).[2] Arguing about the details of how that may be broken simply reveals hardness of heart. Moses gave divorce as a concession, not a 'command' (v 7). Jesus has just been stressing the centrality of forgiveness in personal relationships between citizens of his kingdom.[3] Rather than divorce, the way forward for Christ's disciples lies in forgiveness and restoration of God's original ideal for his good gift of marriage. Only sexual infidelity, breaking the one-flesh union, could be regarded as a legitimate reason for divorce (v 9). While this famous exception guards the rights of the innocent party, even the disciples find it hard to accept (v 10). Jesus responds by showing that for some of his followers it would indeed be better not to marry, because of their predominant commitment to his kingdom.[4]

As if by contrast with a life of celibacy, young children, the fruit of marriage, are brought to Jesus for his blessing (vs 13-15). Contrary to the disciples' false understanding of the low status and unimportance of children, based on their cultural norms, Jesus uses the dependence of little children as a model of what discipleship really is. We are never more 'blessed' than when we are most dependent on him.

The areas where we find God's Word hardest to accept reveal the hardness of our hearts. Lord, help us to submit again, as childlike disciples, to your kingly rule in issues of faithfulness and forgiveness.

---

[1] Ps 95:7,8, NIV [2] *Cf* Matt 5:32; 1 Cor 7:10–16 [3] Matt 18:35 [4] *Cf* 1 Cor 7:1, 7–9,32–35

A QUESTION OF VALUES

'He is no fool who gives what he cannot keep to gain what he cannot lose.'[1]

MATTHEW 19:16–30

Since Christ's kingdom belongs to humbly dependent children (vs 13-15), the wealthy young man stands in stark contrast, for all his splendid record. His fundamental fallacy appears in his initial question, 'What good thing must I do to get …?' (v 16). In reply, Jesus emphasises love for neighbour, but it is love for God which is really the focus of his challenge (v 21). The response revealed that love for possessions ruled his heart, in spite of his outward piety. He knew what he was worth, but regarded its sacrifice as too great a price, because he did not realise Jesus' worth. Indeed, the picture of the camel and the needle's eye shows that it was impossible for him to change. God has to perform a miracle for anyone to receive eternal life (v 26). I cannot do anything to get eternal life.

Again, the disciples are dismayed (v 25). They regarded wealth as a clear sign of God's blessing, so if this rich man cannot enter heaven, can they? But Jesus quickly reassures them that there will be spectacular future rewards for this faithful nucleus of renewed Israel, as ruling elders over the new community (v 28). The test is whether they are willing to endure privations now, in the light of their glorious future. The young man chose the present, and went away sad. The disciples too will run away when Jesus is arrested,[2] though they will return to him later and, eventually, the vision of the Son of Man reigning in glory will come to dominate their lives - as it should do ours.

For we too are potentially included in the promises to 'everyone' who adopts the values of Christ's kingdom (v 29). Sacrifice now for Jesus' sake brings multiple blessings in this world and life in the eternal kingdom. The more despised his faithful disciples are now, the more honoured they will be 'at the renewal of all things' (v 28).[3]

How should the 'renewal of all things' change my natural tendency not to want to give up things in this world for Christ and his kingdom?

[1] Jim Elliot, missionary to the Auca tribe in Ecuador, martyred 1956 [2] See Matt 26:56 [3] Acts 3:21; Eph 1:9,10; Col 1:19,20; 2 Pet 3:10–13

OFFENSIVE GENEROSITY

Think of the most recent evidences of God's undeserved generosity in your own life, and pause to give him thanks.

MATTHEW 20:1–16

The rich young man thought he could buy his way into God's favour, earning heaven by his external righteousness. This is our default position too, because the sinful human heart always seeks to justify itself. So this parable, unique to Matthew, is an exposition of 19:30, repeated at 20:16, and a powerful corrective to our wrong thinking.

The offence of the story is the seeming unfairness of the landowner's behaviour. He pays the same denarius (a day's wage) to the man who has worked from sunrise to sunset and to the man who has worked only the last hour. It is against our sense of natural justice. But actually there is nothing unjust about this, since those who worked the whole day received their agreed wage, in full. The problem is not injustice, but generosity. The labourers of one hour are paid not on the basis of work done (merit), but out of sheer generosity and compassion (grace). That is demonstrated by the way their pay far exceeds the time and energy expended. This is the polar opposite of human religion, which always wants to bargain with God – 'I will do this if you will promise to give me that.'

It's an attitude deep within our own hearts, exposed whenever we become envious of God's generosity towards someone else (v 15). Like the older brother in the parable of the lost son,[1] we can find ourselves resentful, thinking of all we suppose we have done for God and how little we have been appreciated, recognised or rewarded. Immediately, we are putting ourselves at the back of the queue – 'the last'. In Christ's kingdom, grace transcends all our imagined merit or deserving. Instead of whining resentment, let us fix our thoughts on God's amazing grace and goodness in calling us to serve him, and be thankful.

'What do you have that you did not receive? And if you did receive it, why do you boast as though you did not?'[2] Think this through!

---

[1] Luke 15:28–32 [2] 1 Cor 4:7

UPSIDE-DOWN KINGDOM

'Like a servant you came, and if we do the same, we'll be turning the world upside down.'[1] Lord, teach me your new way to be great.

MATTHEW 20:17–28

This passage presents two starkly different ways of understanding Jesus' reign as Messiah, God's King. Approaching Jerusalem, Jesus takes time to explain to his disciples how the Son of Man will come to his throne (vs 17-19). The detail is horrifying – condemnation by Israel's leaders, mockery and torture at the hands of pagans, culminating in the terrifying reality of the one word, 'crucified'. Beyond that lies the resurrection, but that eternal victory requires the ultimate price. For Jesus, the pathway to the crown must pass through the cross. But for James and John, the kingdom is all about authority and power. Jesus has promised a special role for the twelve,[2] but they want to secure a more privileged place for themselves, and their mother's request will surely be hard to refuse (vs 20,21). Glory without suffering attracts us all, of course, but those who would reign with Jesus must drink his cup (v 22). That is the very essence of discipleship – being willing to suffer with Jesus now.[3] 'You' in verse 22 is plural, addressed to all the disciples, for they all have the same problem – as do we.

The ten are indignant (v 24) because they want for themselves what Zebedee's sons have asked for. This competition for status lurks at the very heart of much church leadership (perhaps you can think of a specific example?), but it denies the very nature of Christ's kingdom. Greatness here is measured in terms of service, and the highest attainable status is that of a slave (vs 26,27). It is the pagans who lord it over their people and who crucify the Son of Man. Such lust for power reveals their fundamental self-centredness; they want to be gods. But the Son of Man is a suffering servant, whose death, as substitute and sacrifice for his people's sins, alone can ransom sinners and open the door to everlasting life (v 28).

'Not so with you' (v 26). Where has my thinking about life in the kingdom become 'Gentile'?

[1] P Appleford, 'O Lord, all the world belongs to you' ©1965 J Weinberger Ltd
[2] Matt 19:28   [3] Rom 8:17; 2 Cor 4:10–12

BELIEVING IS SEEING

Lord Jesus, open up my eyes, with truth to free me and light to chase the lies.

MATTHEW 20:29–34

Jericho is the last stop before Jerusalem, the final event before Christ's triumphal entry (21:1-11). This passage centres on the persistent petitions of the blind men, which provide the supreme example of a right approach to Jesus. Unlike the self-seeking of James and John (v 21), these men cry out to Jesus to meet their greatest need and so to change their lives. This small seed of true faith flourishes, in contrast to the selfishness of the disciples and the ignorance of the crowd (v 31). Urgent, persistent petitions remain a key aspect of living faith.

Their use of the titles 'Lord' and 'Son of David' (vs 30,31) also indicate their faith, but Matthew makes clear that the miracle of healing is generated by Christ's compassion (v 34). Here is the Son of Man serving those in desperate need with life-transforming mercy. 'Son of David' had become a Messianic title, based on God's promise to David of an unending dynasty.[1] The beggars may be blind, but they have 'seen' that Jesus is God's eternal King. Once that is grasped, the natural and proper reaction is to cry for mercy, however the crowd may obstruct (v 31). Equally, it is the natural response of this gracious King to stop and meet their faith with mercy and compassion, as he does for them what no one else could do (v 34). No wonder that those whose eyes he opens follow him!

What they would see in the next few days in Jerusalem would be the Son of David coming to his throne through sacrifice, laying down his life in compassion to bring sight to a blinded world. What they had experienced was an enacted picture of the very heart of his mission, which would bring countless others to see and to follow.

How can I better minister the King's compassion in my dealings with friends and family, in church and in the workplace?

[1] 2 Sam 7:11–16

HERE COMES THE KING!

'The Lord needs them' (v 3). Let us lay all that we have and are at the Master's feet today.

MATTHEW 21:1–11

The kingship theme continues with the arrival of the Son of David at his royal city. This enormously significant event marks the beginning of the last section of the Gospel, as the predicted passion of Christ unfolds.[1] Jesus clearly intends to proclaim his identity publicly. He directs all that happens, choosing to fulfil Zechariah 9:9 by riding into the city on a donkey. This is not only a Messianic statement but also an exposition of the nature of his kingly rule. He is the gentle King (v 5), riding in humility, without either sword or army, for he is 'gentle and humble in heart'.[2] He brings rest for the souls of all who submit to his rule, as he subverts all worldly models of authority by his easy yoke. He comes not to be served, but to serve – bringing not conflict, but peace.

The shouts of the crowd all indicate their Messianic expectations. They use royal titles, calling on God to rescue his people now, quoting the great Passover psalm[3] with its theme of salvation. The garments spread in the road and the branches from the trees (v 8) confirm that this is a statement of kingly rule – highly dangerous to the Roman occupation and their Sadducean allies. So Matthew uses a striking verb to describe Jerusalem's response (v 10). He will use it again in 27:51. This is a seismic event, which shakes Jerusalem to its very foundations.

And yet… the crowd's identification of Jesus as merely 'the prophet from Nazareth' (v 11) is disappointing. They may mean that he is the prophet like Moses, who was to come.[4] He is also the King, like David who called his greater descendant 'Lord'.[5] But the Word of God on his lips will be rejected and the Son of David will be cast out of his city, shaken though it is. The world prefers its rebellion.

Consider 2 Corinthians 10:1–6. How can we subvert the power-hungry structures of this rebellious world by the gentleness and meekness of Christ?

[1] Matt 20:18,19 [2] *See* Matt 11:29 [3] Ps 118:26 [4] Deut 18:15 [5] Matt 22:42–45

DAY OF VISITATION

'Cleanse me from my sin, Lord ... make my heart your palace and your royal throne.'[1]

MATTHEW 21:12–17

Having entered his city, the Son of David goes at once to its heart, the temple. Four centuries earlier, Malachi had prophesied that the Lord would suddenly come to his temple, to refine and purify, but asked, 'Who can stand when he appears?'[2] The gentle King now exercises his authority in a symbolic action of upheaval, indicating that because the temple's purpose is so abased, its very existence is threatened.

This is not primarily a protest about economic exploitation, since Jesus ejects both buyers and sellers. It is a spiritual judgement, because the place of prayer for all the nations (the outer court of the Gentiles) has been turned into a market. As in Jeremiah's time, God's people are deluded in thinking that because the temple bears God's name they are 'safe to do all these detestable things.'[3] The 'den of robbers' reference exposes those who rob God of his true glory by finding their imagined security in formal religion, while in reality their hearts are far from him.

By contrast, verses 14 and 15 picture the proper use of the temple – to heal the blind and the lame and to hear the praises of little ones who recognise the King. Christ's compassion enables the handicapped, who would have been confined to the outer court, to meet with God in the temple itself, having been made whole. Jesus is providing the access to God that the temple was designed to provide. He is the true Son of David, whose praises on the children's lips silence God's enemies.[4] Indeed, that is precisely what happened as Jesus left the religious leaders that evening. They could hardly be in doubt as to how 'the prophet from Nazareth' viewed them, but soon he would declare to them, 'Your house is left to you desolate' (23:38).

'Lord, help me to search out those parts of my life where false confidence in external religion has replaced heart-repentance and true obedience to your kingly rule.'

[1] R Hudson Pope, *CSSM Choruses 18*, alt [2] Mal 3:1–3 [3] *See* Jer 7:9–11
[4] *See* Ps 8:2

THE POWER OF JESUS' WORDS

'Faith comes from hearing the message ... through the word about Christ.'[1] Lord, help me to listen today.

MATTHEW 21:18–22

The arrival of God's King in his city is a time of crisis, or judgement. In the Bible, whenever God comes he does so to save his believing people, but also to judge his enemies. The attitude of individuals towards the King and his rule indicates into which category they are placing themselves. That division, seen in the temple (vs 12-17), is still the same today.

This passage presents a striking contrast between the withered fig tree (vs 19,20) and the buoyant faith of verses 21 and 22. Jesus pronounces judgement on the tree, because it has failed to produce figs, which is its purpose. Leaves alone are deceptive and inadequate. Fruitlessness means that it no longer deserves to live (v 19). This is a solemn use of Christ's divine power, but it is immediately effective. For the same Lord who heals and saves also judges and destroys, and the whole ministry of Jesus must be understood in this light. The miracle has significance firstly as a warning to Christ's enemies. The fig tree frequently appears in the Old Testament as an image for Israel, whose impending judgement Jesus increasingly pronounces.[2] Failure to repent and believe the gospel of the kingdom will inevitably lead to destruction.

But the miracle also provides great encouragement to Christ's disciples to express their faith in believing prayer (v 22). Clearly, cursing trees and moving mountains[3] are not to be the literal ingredients of their ministries, or ours; but seeing God do the 'impossible'[4] in response to believing prayer truly is. When Jesus departs, the channels of divine power will always remain open to praying believers who ask in faith, however impossible the request may seem to be. They still are.

Are there any areas of life where I have given up asking because I have given up believing? How should this word of Christ grow my faith?

---

[1] Rom 10:17 [2] *See* Matt 21:43; 23:37–39 [3] *Cf* Zech 4:6,7 [4] *Cf* Matt 19:26

THE ISSUE OF AUTHORITY

'Lord, cure me of my intermittent piety and make me thoroughly Christian.'[1]

MATTHEW 21:23–27

As Jesus returns to the temple courts to resume his primary ministry of teaching, the conflict quickly resurfaces. The decisive struggle begins here and runs through to the end of chapter 23. His whole ministry has taught the Word of God and revealed, in his own person, God's kingly rule, only to be met with rejection. Now, the highest representatives of the establishment directly question his authority (v 23), prompted by the cleansing of the temple, the previous day. This is their turf!

Jesus counters their question with one of his own about John the Baptist (vs 24,25). The question is neither theoretical nor merely clever; it is a devastating exposure of their hypocrisy. They had steadfastly resisted John's baptism (John's 'you brood of vipers' is repeated by Jesus)[2] – even though the people, including Jesus himself, had obeyed his call. Having refused the forerunner, they are now about to reject the Messiah himself and crucify him. What really exposes their duplicity is their discussion about how to reply (vs 25,26). It has nothing to do with truth and everything to do with preserving their own position, justifying their disobedience and at all costs retaining their authority and status with the people. Such prevarication can only produce the pitifully weak response, 'We don't know' (v 27). It is always the last refuge of human religiosity with all its empty self-seeking when confronted by the authoritative Word of the living God.

Although they know the right answer, they refuse to give it, so instead of answering them, Jesus tells the parable of the two sons (vs 28-32), by which he nails their stubborn refusal to repent and believe either John's message or his own.

Hypocrisy and dissembling are the outcome of disobedience, itself the product of unbelief. Where do I need freshly to trust and obey Jesus, to rid myself of my mask-wearing?

[1] John Wesley, founder of Methodism, 1703–91 [2] Matt 3:7; 12:34

WORDS AND DEEDS

O God, we cannot pretend before you. Help us to read this passage honestly, and show us ourselves within it.

MATTHEW 21:28–32

'What do you think?' (v 28). The first son answered his father disrespectfully, 'I will not', while the other son, appearing polite and deferential (his answer, literally translated is 'Here I am, Lord') apparently puts himself into his father's hands. Then comes the twist. The 'good' son disobeys; the 'bad' son changes his mind and goes. Which son's statement more accurately reflects our verbal response to God? Neil Hood asks of the second son, 'What was his problem? Did he forget? Was he too busy? Did he never intend to go in the first place? Or did he mean to go, but hadn't counted the cost?'[1]

The parable is of course aimed in the first instance at the chief priests and elders who had just challenged Jesus' right to act and teach as he did (v 23). This parable is not about who will 'go to heaven', for the kingdom of God was a present reality. The problem for the religious establishment was that it was being peopled by the scum of society, who listened, repented and believed what John the Baptist had to say.

This parable, and others in this section of Matthew with a similar theme, is often misread as though Jesus was saying that the tax collectors and prostitutes would enter the kingdom while the religious leaders would not. But no. The question is who has priority in the kingdom. The answer is all those who believe and repent, even those who come late to faith, and obey. We might take note that, historically, that includes all of us who are Gentiles.

Incidentally, I have often had cause to remember this parable at its most uncomplicated level. It is always better to say 'No' and then surprise someone than to say 'Yes' and fail them. It is better to tell someone 'I prayed for you this week' than to promise to pray – and then forget.

Do you need to act on some unkept promise?

[1] Neil Hood, *Whose Life is it Anyway?*, Authentic, 2003

WHOSE VINEYARD IS IT?

Lord, we put ourselves into your hands today, remembering that we are your servants.

MATTHEW 21:33–46

This second 'vineyard' parable is an extension of the allegory in Isaiah 5:1-7, with a change of emphasis. Jesus adds the factor of the tenants and the absentee landlord. Like the previous parable, it is addressed in the first instance to the religious stakeholders of the day, and with the prophecies fulfilled, including the murder-execution of the owner's son, it is not hard to see the point that Jesus was making (*see also* v 45). Both parables are concerned with fruitfulness. This parable also ends with a declaration of the reversal that God will bring about. Don't miss the irony of verse 46 – Jesus has just prophesied his own arrest, for which prophecy the chief priests and elders looked for a way to arrest him!

I think the parable has a second meaning for us today. What was the problem with the tenant farmers? The issue at the heart of the story – for the Pharisees as well as for us – is that the tenants had forgotten whose vineyard it was in the first place. They murdered the first three servants because they wanted to enjoy the wine. They murder the owner's son because they now want his inheritance as well.

There is a warning here for all of us who work as tenants in God's vineyard against thinking of the vineyard as our own. If we forget that we are stewards we are prone to temptations of many kinds. We may try to exercise control over others, or exclude those whom we see as undesirable. We may congratulate ourselves on our success or despair at our failure. We forget that the owner will return, and will demand an accounting. These things happen in the church and they happen in families. None of us has proprietary ownership of the kingdom of heaven.

Lord, help us to live in freedom as your servants.

KINGDOM DRESS CODE

Lord, call us aside from our preoccupations to listen to you.

MATTHEW 22:1–14

Here we have the third parable addressed to the very people at whose hands Jesus knew he was about to be killed.[1] The point is very much the same as that of the two earlier parables, that these members of the religious establishment were in danger of excluding themselves from the kingdom, but here the problem addressed is different. Just as the son (21:30) failed to act on his words and the tenant farmers forgot that they were stewards, so the wedding guests were too preoccupied with their own affairs.

Unique to Matthew's telling of the story is the curious ending in verses 11 and 12. If you are like me your immediate response is: 'But that's unfair. How could someone brought in off the street be expected to have proper dress for a wedding?' We too are speechless at his treatment – but wait. Matthew himself was a tax collector, or had been until he met Jesus! He knew from experience that what is required from disciples is a radical righteousness, a standard which neither he nor any of us can ever meet on our own. All the guests must have been provided with clothes to wear. So what is the problem with the man who was thrown out? He failed to realise, just like the first invitees, the brilliance of this occasion and turned aside his host's gracious provision. He thought he could come in his old clothes.

Yes, tax collectors and prostitutes enter the kingdom before the religious leaders – but once inside they are tax collectors and prostitutes no longer. The dress code is the same for us all; and none of us can provide our own. Many (v 14) receive invitations; but only those who come appropriately dressed are allowed in.

How seriously are you taking your invitation to the great banquet? Does your 'field' or your 'business' crowd out your appreciation of what God has prepared?[2]

---

[1] Matt 16:21   [2] 1 Cor 2:9,10

WHEN THE LAW IS UNJUST

Remember as you approach this passage that you bear the image of God, and praise him for it.

MATTHEW 22:15–22

The Pharisees sent their disciples to Jesus, together with some supporters of Herod. (We can only speculate why they did not confront him themselves.) The question of the taxes to Caesar was designed to make Jesus incriminate himself whichever way he answered. If he said 'Yes', he would be aligning himself with Herod and the hated Romans; if 'No', he would be winning favour with the crowds who were burdened by overtaxation, but he could be accused of fomenting a revolution against the Romans. The Pharisees also hoped to force Jesus to take sides in their disagreement with the Sadducees over the legitimacy of using political means to further their religious ends.

Knowing what was in their minds, Jesus responded with another question, avoiding their trap while not avoiding the issue. The imperial coin was stamped with the image of the emperor and the legend 'Tiberius Caesar, son of the divine Augustus'. Despite the inscription, Jesus affirms the requirement to keep the law, while teaching that there are situations in which obedience to God must take priority,[1] thereby turning a particular issue for that time into one for all disciples.[2] He wants us to think about what is Caesar's and what is God's. There are no easy answers!

Two principles are clear. First, Christians are not absolved (by virtue of their membership in God's kingdom) from civic responsibility. Second, when that clashes with obedience to God, his command takes priority. The two are not parallel, but responsibility to the authorities is subsumed under our responsibility to God. Jesus' answer raises the issue to a much more difficult plane. We are stamped with the image of our Lord. What are the implications for our use of time and talents, for our attitudes, priorities, decisions, and the direction of our lives?

Pray for Christians who live under unjust jurisdictions, that they may live faithfully as citizens of the kingdom.

[1] Acts 4:19; 5:29 [2] Rom 13:6,7; 1 Pet 2:13–17

POWER BIBLE STUDY

'Lord, open my eyes so that my Bible reading comes alive.'[1]

MATTHEW 22:23–33

It is now the turn of the Sadducees, who resort to a rabbinic method of argument: making the beliefs of an opponent appear ridiculous. The Sadducees recognised only the Pentateuch. Their question is based on the law of levirate marriage (from Latin *levir*, 'brother-in-law'), the responsibility of a man to marry his widowed sister-in-law.[2] The purpose of this law was to preserve the continuity of inheritance, especially land, within the same family, a principle fundamental to the Jewish economy. The Sadducees doubtless thought it was a clever question. Jesus' answer was devastating. Can you imagine a greater put-down?

How do we read God's word? Paul urged Timothy to take great pains as he studied the Bible, handling it correctly.[3] The unusual word used here (*orthotomeo*) means literally 'cutting a straight path' and suggests that the Bible teacher should aim to guide people straight to the goal. It precludes the byways of nitpicking debates and interpretations that do not build people up in justice, mercy and faithfulness.[4] We need to be reading the Scriptures for ourselves, like the Bereans,[5] systematically and regularly. We need to read the whole Bible, interpreting scripture by scripture. (The word 'heresy' comes from a Greek word which means 'picking and choosing'.) We need to read the difficult parts, becoming familiar with the background of the Bible and understanding how the details fit into the major themes. We need to understand the different genres of literature in its 66 books, and the different ways that they need to be approached and understood. Above all, we should constantly seek to apply what we read to our current situation. Jesus also warns that understanding of Scripture needs to be matched by an ever-present experience of the power of God (v 29) – resurrection power.[6]

Ask yourself whether your habit of Bible study is matched by a living experience of the power of God.

[1] Ps 119:18, adapted [2] Deut 25:5 – 6:3 [3] 2 Tim 2:15 [4] Matt 23:23 [5] Acts 17:11 [6] *Compare* Eph 1:18–21; Phil 3:10

THE HEART OF THE MATTER

Father, open my eyes to your love so that I may reflect it to others around me.

MATTHEW 22:34–46

The Pharisees, gloating in Jesus' ability to silence their opponents, take up the argument, grandstanding on their superior understanding of the Scriptures. The question they ask is not entirely a theoretical one, since their own teachers distinguished between 'light' and 'heavy' commandments, and even Jesus referred to 'weightier' commandments.[1] If this was intended as a way of scoring points against their fellows, Jesus took the issue seriously, answering it in one of his most memorable sayings.

Most of us, I imagine, have had the experience of being attacked by unbelievers who think they can dismiss the Christian faith by ridicule, impressive knowledge, clever arguments and the like. I have often been caught off my guard at such times. Jesus' response to the Pharisees suggests that there are ways in which we can seize these moments. Notice that he was not dismissive of their questions, even though they were posed to trap him. Neither was he intimidated. Poise on these difficult occasions comes from confidence in our faith, and is cultivated by honesty with ourselves. Often our detractors have a point, and we should graciously acknowledge that and take note. We need never be afraid that arguments will tear down the kingdom of God. 'Defend the Bible?' asked Charles Spurgeon. 'I'd as soon defend a lion.' All truth is God's truth, whether found in the Bible or a biology research laboratory. Often our thinking is not sophisticated enough to resolve all the apparent problems, but that should lead to humility, not arrogance. Searching online, I was saddened to find websites in which Christians battle for their position on some particular issue, showing little love and much self-righteousness. Even if we don't have Jesus' debating skills, a life lived in his risen power will point to our Saviour when arguments fail.

How can you be ready to give an answer to someone who challenges your faith?

1 eg Matt 23:23, NRSV

THE PERILS OF PEDESTALS

'Thou who wast rich beyond all splendour / All for love's sake becamest poor. / Thrones for a manger didst surrender, / Sapphire-paved courts for stable floor.'[1]

MATTHEW 23:1–22

This section falls into two halves: in the first part Jesus is speaking to the crowds; in the second he addresses the Pharisees directly. It may come as a surprise that he tells the crowds to obey all that they teach, but the intentions of the Pharisees were excellent, inasmuch as they pursued and taught righteousness. Jesus had also just made it plain (in the incident with the coin) that earthly leaders are in principle to be obeyed. However, many of the Pharisees did not practise what they preached, and missed the forest of mercy, justice and humility for the trees of quibbles about the law.

It is all too easy for us to think that we would never behave like the Pharisees – just as they, in turn, thought that they would never commit the sins of their forefathers (v 30). Christian leaders are prone to the particular temptations of their office. Eugene Peterson brings verses 6 and 7 into our culture by paraphrasing: 'They love to sit at the head table at church dinners, basking in the most prominent positions, preening in the radiance of public flattery, receiving honorary degrees, and getting called "Doctor" and "Reverend."'[2] Ouch.

What would Jesus have to say about authoritarianism in our churches? Are we telling people how to live their lives, teaching selectively, focusing on ethical issues in which we personally are not tempted (homosexuality and abortion come to mind), while skating over other issues (divorce, greed), which may touch us closer to home; holding out condemnation where mercy is indicated, and generally shutting the kingdom in people's faces? The Bible has high standards in these areas, which we must teach and uphold. At the same time we are called to model what we teach, never forgetting that we are all brothers and sisters in constant need of forgiveness.

'The greatest among you will be your servant' (v 11). Pray about how these words apply to your everyday life.

[1] Frank Houghton, missionary bishop in China, 1894–1972 [2] *The Message*

SNAKES!

Let the searching light of the Spirit shine into the inmost recesses of your heart. He loves you.

MATTHEW 23:23–39

'You snakes!' We are reminded of the cunning deceiver of Genesis 3:1-5. Donald Hagner calls this passage (and the previous one), with its repeated woes, 'certainly one of the most, if not the most, painful in the NT.'[1] We do not expect such violent confrontation from Jesus. He exposes the hypocrisy of the Pharisees in stinging words and vivid images. He accuses them – yes, the Pharisees who so prided themselves on keeping the law – of *akrasia*, lack of self-control (v 25), *akatharsia*, uncleanness (v 27) and *anomia*, lawlessness (TNIV 'wickedness', v 28). In so doing he cuts at the heart of their understanding of holiness and defines it in a radically new way.

Jesus' castigation of hypocrisy suggests a checklist for Christian leaders: Do I have friends and mentors to help me stay honest? How do I support those who are struggling? Do I practise what I teach, week by week? Is my relationship with all other Christians that of a brother or sister? Do I feed on praise? What do I do to make sure that I don't lose sight of the weightier issues? Am I careful to be Christlike in the details of my life? Am I concerned about my image? What kind of a role model am I?

This section ends with one of the tenderest passages in the New Testament, as Jesus, practising what he preaches, shows himself to be full of justice and mercy. His standards are uncompromising. There is a time limit to God's offer of forgiveness,[2] and his mercy is no excuse for presumption. At the same time, his compassion is boundless. Biblical teaching on judgement has over the centuries tended to err either by emphasising God's wrath or his mercy to the exclusion of the other. To be faithful to the Scriptures we must teach both. This chapter helps us to keep them in balance.

Make the checklist above a matter for prayer. Are there other questions you might add, based on this passage and the previous one?

[1] DA Hagner, *Matthew 14–28*, WBC 33B; Word Books, 1995, p672
[2] Rom 2:2–5

HOPE IN THE DARKEST TIMES

Jesus saw the need to prepare his followers for the trials and struggles ahead. Pray that we too might understand his words and be faithful to him.

MATTHEW 24:1–14

The opening words of this chapter should be read in relation to the moving passage in 23:37–39. Within that context the statement that Jesus 'left the temple and was walking away' carries terrible significance, both for the temple and for the Jewish people. The disciples' attempt to draw Christ's attention to the external glory of Jerusalem suggests disbelief of his announcement of a coming desolation for this city. They seek clarification and reassurance.

Jesus provides the former but not the latter: 'not one stone here will be left on another.' The city and its temple (which was believed to be indestructible) are defenceless because, with the rejection of the Messiah and his kingdom, the glory of God is departing.[1] In a world becoming overwhelmingly urban, perhaps there is a warning for us: no city can provide its inhabitants with security on the basis of past or present glories when its social life is characterised by injustice and evil.

Jesus now ceases public ministry and concentrates on preparing his disciples for lives of obedience to him in a world that will often seem chaotic and dangerous. What he says to them (and us) may be summed up as follows: seek discernment – the passage warns about the danger of being deceived and the need to avoid fruitless speculation concerning the future (vs 4–6); practise perseverance – the message of the kingdom must be taken to 'all nations' (v 14), but this will involve hardship and suffering and will require the disciples to 'stand firm to the end' (*see* v 13); never abandon hope – the history of the world will be tragic and violent, but the disciple-community knows that this is 'the beginning of birth-pains' (v 8). Since the coming of Christ, the history of the world is not finally meaningless; even now we witness a great transformation.

Jesus anticipates that when troubles come 'the love of most will grow cold'. Pray that your love for Christ and for people will not fail the test.

[1] *See Ezek 11:22–25*

LIVING THROUGH TERROR

Christ warns of coming terror, but he also predicts the global spread of the kingdom of God. Pray to be able to see beyond our immediate fears to what is promised.

MATTHEW 24:15–35

This passage and the one that follows have given interpreters of the Bible many problems. This means that we should approach them carefully and humbly, willing to admit that some of Christ's words may be unclear to us. Remember that Jesus is here responding to two separate questions from his disciples. First, they have asked him when the terrible destruction of Jerusalem and its temple will occur. Secondly, they ask a different question: what will be the signs of the end of the world (v 3)? In today's passage, Jesus appears to respond to the first question before moving on to the enquiry concerning his final coming. He indicates that the destruction of Jerusalem, with the terrible sufferings that would accompany it, is imminent, since everything predicted in this passage will happen before this generation passes away (v 34). In AD 70 the Roman armies did indeed destroy Jerusalem.

However, the events predicted here will result in a great extension of the kingdom of God, as appointed preachers (the word often translated 'angels' in verse 31 can also mean 'messengers') take the news of God's grace into all the world. Once again the light of hope breaks through the darkness of the storms immediately ahead with the promise that God's elect will be drawn 'from one end of the heavens to the other' (v 31) – apocalyptic language with a this-worldly application.

The language used by Jesus in this passage ('flee', 'great distress', 'the distress of those days') suggests the coming of a time of terror. We also live at a time when such language has become familiar, as many people face great insecurity and distress. Now, as then, our only true defence against evil is found in Jesus and his teaching: 'Heaven and earth will pass away, but my words will never pass away' (v 35).

The passage describes people in flight from violence and devastation; remember those who are refugees today and pray that they may find hope beyond terror.

GET READY!

Help us, Lord Jesus, never to lose sight of the horizon of hope that is the promise of your coming, and enable us to live all our lives in readiness for that great day.

MATTHEW 24:36–51

Jesus now turns to the second question asked by his disciples: what will be the sign of your coming and the end of the age? Whereas he answered their first query with clear indications of what lay in the immediate future, his reply regarding the time of his final coming is characterised by mystery. The contrast between the two passages could hardly be greater: where the previous section encouraged reading the 'signs of the times' (vs 32,33), Jesus now states that the timing of the end is unknown even to himself (v 36).

This is a remarkable text, which suggests the absurdity of all human speculation concerning the time of the end. If the Father has reserved this information for himself, then the matter is closed and any attempt to devise a prophetic timetable is an act of disobedience because it ignores Christ's explicit teaching. However, while the timing remains uncertain, the event itself is not, and this results in repeated instructions concerning the need to 'keep watch' (v 42), be 'ready' (v 44), and be 'faithful' (v 45). What is more, faithfulness is defined by Jesus in terms of serving other people. We prepare for the end not by keeping an eye on the prophetic clock but by providing for the needs of others.

Jesus draws a parallel with the times of Noah (vs 37-39). Noah's contemporaries were simply too busy enjoying life to think of anything beyond the immediate present. The same temptation faces us as Christians, especially in a world saturated with messages and images that wipe out the promise of the Lord's coming, creating a view of life in which there is, quite literally, no end in sight. This is why the early Christians constantly reminded each other of this horizon by using the greeting, Maranatha – 'Our Lord, come!'[1]

How, practically, can you keep the hope of the coming of the Lord alive as a guiding principle in your life and work?

[1] 1 Cor 16:22

HOLY IMPATIENCE

Lord Jesus, give us such a love for you and commitment to your honour that we may always be ready for the midnight cry announcing your coming.

MATTHEW 25:1–13

The message we have heard from Jesus in the previous chapter is now driven home by three parables, each of which underlines the importance of being ready for the coming of the Lord. In this passage Christ vividly describes a traditional village wedding ceremony in which the arrival of the bridegroom is unaccountably delayed (v 5). Jesus has already indicated that God's elect must be gathered 'from the four winds,'[1] so the delay in the coming of the bridegroom is not really surprising. At the end of this Gospel the risen Christ sends the apostles to 'all nations' with a commission to disciple them,[2] a task that might suggest that the bridegroom will be a 'long time in coming' (v 5).

The original readers of Matthew's Gospel in the second half of the first century may often have asked why the final coming of the kingdom of God seemed to be so long delayed. Why was the bridegroom keeping everyone waiting so long?[3] Two thousand years later we may sometimes ask that same question. Such questioning is not necessarily contrary to faith: there is such a thing as 'holy impatience' – a deep longing that the cries of the godly across the ages will finally be answered with the arrival of God's kingdom. The very last prayer in the Bible breathes this spirit of holy impatience with its longing for the bridegroom's appearance: 'The Spirit and the bride say, "Come!"'[4] Notice the warning in this parable, however: the delay in the appearance of the bridegroom exposes the lack of preparation made by some of the participants in the ceremony and leads to their humiliation and great loss. The story serves once again to highlight Jesus' message: 'keep watch, because you do not know the day or the hour' (v 13).

Think about the phrase 'holy impatience'. Does it describe the way you pray for the world?

[1] Matt 24:31 [2] *See* Matt 28:16–20 [3] 2 Pet 3:3–9 [4] Rev 22:17

WHAT IS FAITHFULNESS?

The treasure of the gospel does not need conserving, but rather releasing to do its transforming work. Deliver us, Lord, from the stupidity of burying this treasure beneath the debris of our traditions.

MATTHEW 25:14–30

This story presents us with some very startling imagery involving what might be called 'big business'. And it really is big! The chief executive in question entrusts his managers with huge funds and looks for substantial returns on his investments. Once again the theme of a long delay in the coming of the day of reckoning surfaces when we are told that the master returned 'after a long time' (v 19). Attention focuses on the manager who failed to put his employer's money to use and simply returned the capital sum without addition.

It should be obvious that the parable is not designed to instruct us in either economic science or business management. Jesus uses vivid illustrations drawn from real life without necessarily endorsing all the practices he refers to. The key question is: how would the disciples have understood this story? Was the manager who was satisfied simply to conserve the treasure entrusted to him representative of the Jewish leaders? Had they not been given the riches of God's Word and effectively buried it within their traditions, preventing it from multiplying blessings among the people? And are the disciples therefore being warned not to do something similar with the gospel when the return of Christ seems to be delayed?

There is a searching warning here. What does it mean to remain faithful to Jesus? This parable suggests that it involves unleashing the full power of the treasures God has entrusted to us. The message of the gospel has not been left with the church in order that it might simply be conserved; it needs to be released into the world in the way the Master clearly intends (vs 21,23). If we fail to understand this and confuse faithfulness with mere conservation, then the warnings with which this story concludes (v 30) present us with a terrible challenge.

Think about the ways in which we may fall into the trap of the foolish servant, and ask to be delivered from such tragic errors.

THE END OF THE STORY

'Father, please give us a faith that "works by love" so that when the Great Day comes we may inherit the kingdom prepared for the saints "since the creation of the world."'[1]

MATTHEW 25:31–46

Jesus' instruction to his disciples concerning the end of the world reaches a wonderful climax with this final parable. There is no ambiguity about the scene here: the 'delay' is over as the Son of Man 'comes in his glory' and 'all the nations' are 'gathered before him' (v 31).

Now a separation takes place, as the sheep are divided from the goats. The basis on which this momentous decision is made concerns human behaviour – whether or not the hungry were fed and cared for, the lonely given shelter and companionship, the sick and prisoners visited (vs 35,36, and 42,43). As Joachim Jeremias puts it: 'At the Last Judgement God will look for a faith that has been lived-out.'[2] To the astonished reaction of the righteous, who were simply unaware of serving the King when doing what came naturally to them, he replies that what they did in serving 'the least of these brothers and sisters of mine, you did for me' (v 40).

Scholars debate who is meant by 'these brothers and sisters of mine'. Some restrict it to the disciples, so that evidence of belonging to the kingdom is found in the response made to the servants of Christ. However, the scene described at the beginning of the story involving 'all the nations', and the teaching of Jesus that becoming like the heavenly Father means reflecting his love for all, including 'enemies',[3] suggest a much wider reference and a broader conception of God's grace. There is, though, a clear division as those who failed to show mercy and compassion are told to depart 'into the eternal fire prepared for the devil and his angels' (v 41). Notice carefully what is said here: God desires the salvation of all people and provides for their deliverance; those who close their hearts to his love and persist in evil choose a destiny that was not intended for them.

This parable is deeply challenging. Consider what a 'lived-out faith' involving practical care for people in need might mean for you.[4]

---

1 See Gal 5:6; Matt 25:34 **2** J Jeremias, *The Parables of Jesus*, SCM, 1972, p209 **3** Matt 5:43–48 **4** James 1:27; 2:14–17

MONEY TO BURN?

Lord, help us understand the blessedness of the woman in this story and give to us the same extravagant love for you, the crucified Messiah.

MATTHEW 26:1–16

With this passage we move from the teaching of Jesus concerning the end times to his actions prior to his death. This transition is clearly indicated in the first two verses with the statement that he 'finished' his teaching and announced that he was soon to be 'handed over to be crucified'. Here, then, we enter holy ground.

The narrative gives us a glimpse of the action taking place in the palace of the high priest (vs 3–5), before switching back to a home in the village of Bethany, where we notice two utterly different reactions to Jesus. First, 'a woman' (identified by John as Mary, the sister of Martha and Lazarus)[1] expresses her love for Christ in an extravagant act of public devotion, pouring expensive perfume over his head. The disciples (led by Judas, according to John 12:4–6) are scandalised by this over-the-top display, pointing out that the money involved might have been 'given to the poor' (vs 8,9). This seems ethically sound, and may even connect with the thrust of the parable in the previous chapter.[2] But Jesus emphatically rejects the criticism: ethical purity becomes hard and unlovely when it blinds us to profound spiritual truth and prevents spontaneous and beautiful acts of devotion and worship.

The second reaction is prompted not by love but by bitterness and hatred (vs 14–16). Once again, money is involved but instead of being spent on Christ it is received as payment for the betrayal of Christ. Both actions anticipate the death of Jesus, but where one penetrates to the deepest meaning of his sacrifice and expresses adoring love, the other is exposed as a squalid act prompted by the desire for personal monetary gain.

How does my attitude towards money indicate my spiritual condition and my relationship to the crucified Jesus?

[1] John 12:1–3 [2] Matt 25:35

KNOWING CHRIST TRULY

Lord Jesus, as we consider the meaning of your sacrifice, help us to feel deeply both our own weakness and your patient grace.

Three things are very striking in this description of Jesus' preparations to celebrate the Passover with his disciples. First, his sense of control over events: he calmly makes the arrangements to eat the Passover meal with his followers and says, 'My appointed time is near' (v 18). Here is clear evidence that his life was not taken from him without his consent; rather, he gave himself freely within the redemptive purposes of the Father.[1]

Secondly, there is a fascinating reference to 'a certain man' within the city with whom some previous arrangement seems to have been made for the use of a room for precisely this purpose. This person has recognised Jesus as 'The Teacher', so we may regard him as an anonymous disciple. In the simple (but probably highly risky) act of making his house available to the Master, this unknown person provided a setting for the institution of the Lord's Supper, and so placed millions of Christians down the centuries in his debt.

Finally, notice the reaction of the disciples to the alarming information that one of them was to betray the Lord (v 21). Matthew informs us that they were all 'very sad' and asked, 'Surely not I, Lord?' All, that is, except one: Judas remained silent and only later joins in the questioning in order not to be isolated (v 25). It is significant too that when the betrayer addresses Jesus it is as Rabbi, rather than Lord. Those who know Christ for who he truly is are aware of their unworthiness and vulnerability, whereas those who never advance beyond a surface knowledge of Jesus remain independent and self-confident. In reality it is they who are in mortal danger.

Consider the difference between knowing Jesus as Rabbi and as Lord, and reflect on the implications for you of confessing him as the latter.

---

[1] John 10:17,18

THE POWER OF MEMORY

Father God, please help us to overcome the danger of familiarity with the words of Jesus and enable us to really hear his message.

MATTHEW 26:26–35

The meal which Jesus here shares with his disciples was the ritual celebration of the Passover (vs 18,19). The blessing of the bread (v 26) and the singing of 'a hymn' (v 30) reflect the traditional structure of this meal, in which the Jewish people recalled the great acts of God which had delivered them from slavery and formed them into a covenant community. However, while Jesus observes the familiar pattern of the Passover meal, he adds words that are startlingly new, using the bread and wine as symbols of his coming death (vs 26–28), so providing a fresh interpretation 'of a new and greater deliverance'.[1] Notice too that the backward reference is matched by a forward look, anticipating the transformation that the death of Jesus will bring about, a transformation that will be complete in his 'Father's kingdom' (v 29).

For many Christians the language of 'the Lord's Supper' is so familiar that its links to the story of Israel are often overlooked, and it becomes difficult to see how it connects to everyday realities in the world. Have we now moved away from concerns with history and politics into a sacred sphere that is sealed off from such everyday matters? The mention of 'the Father's kingdom' connects the death of Christ 'for the forgiveness of sins' (v 28) to all that has gone before. The great redemption about to be accomplished will bring into being a new community, whose members will live by kingdom values. Seen in this light, the Lord's Supper is no privatised religious ritual, but rather a celebration of the Saviour whose death and resurrection provide the dynamic to resist evil, to live in hope of the coming of the Lord, and to offer the world an alternative way of being human in which the hungry are fed, strangers are cared for, and the sick and imprisoned are visited.[2]

Think about the dangers of failing to connect the Lord's table to the reality of life in the world, especially when you next take Communion.

[1] RT France, *Matthew*, TNTC; IVP, 1985, p368 [2] Matt 25:34–36

A WINDOW ON THE CROSS

Thank you, Father God, that we are privileged to listen to the prayers of Jesus; help us to learn from him how truly to pray.

MATTHEW 26:36–46

As we are admitted to the Garden of Gethsemane and witness the agonies of the Son of God, we tread on ground where human language fails and the only adequate response is one of awestruck wonder. According to John, this was a place often frequented by Jesus and his followers, so Judas knew exactly where to find Christ.[1] The narrative (which presumably owes its origin to the recollections shared with the apostles by the risen Lord) allows us to listen to the most intimate prayers of Jesus and provides us with a kind of window through which to gain understanding of the meaning of the cross.

Concerning his prayers: they are uttered by a man in the most extreme state of distress; Hebrews says that Jesus prayed 'with fervent cries and tears'.[2] This explains his felt need for companionship; the three apostles who had been privileged to glimpse his glory in transfiguration might have been expected to stand alongside him in this moment of humiliation. Jesus' intercession in Gethsemane gives us freedom to question the Father, and to do so with passion; but it also suggests that when the wrestling with God is over and his will becomes clear, the search for alternatives must give way to submission. How much prayer is found wanting beside this supreme standard?

Concerning the meaning of the cross: the terrible struggle in the garden clearly indicates the enormity of the burden that was to be borne on Calvary where, as Jesus had indicated at the Passover meal, his blood was to be 'poured out for many for the forgiveness of sins'. But Gethsemane also shows us the profound depths of the love of God and unveils an aspect of his being that is as shocking as it is wonderful. If, as Paul says, the glory of God has been shown to us 'in the face of Christ,'[3] then the portrait in Gethsemane shows that face covered in tears.

Try to find space today to reread this passage and simply meditate on the extraordinary picture it presents of the incarnate Son of God.

[1] John 18:2 [2] Heb 5:7 [3] 2 Cor 4:6

THE SWORD AND THE CROSS

Men of violence arrested the 'Prince of Peace'; help us, Father, to know how to follow him in our 'age of terror'.

MATTHEW 26:47–56

The drama of redemption now moves rapidly towards its climax. The silence of Gethsemane is suddenly shattered by the arrival of an armed gang, led by Judas. Once again the betrayer addresses Jesus with the term Rabbi, only this time the title, accompanied by a mocking kiss, seems ironic and effectively terminates the relationship with Christ. Was Judas motivated by factors other than the love of money? Were his expectations of what the Messiah would accomplish, with hopes of a nationalist and violent movement of insurrection, disappointed by the ministry of Jesus? If so, the actions of Christ in what follows must have strengthened Judas in his disillusion and rejection of the way of Jesus.

With the arrest of Jesus, one of his disciples[1] attempted to resist the officials with armed force, only to be rebuked by Christ and told, 'Put your sword back in its place' (v 52). This repudiation of violence is consistent with the teaching Jesus had given from the beginning of his ministry, since love for enemies and the refusal to return blow for blow had been a central part of his instruction of his disciples.[2] The ancient world was characterised by terrible violence, both that inflicted by the state and the violence of revolutionary reaction. In this situation Jesus taught his followers how to break out of this vicious circle, and for the best part of three hundred years, Christians understood peacemaking to be a distinguishing mark of discipleship.[3] Clearly, the central point here is that, having committed himself to the Father's will in Gethsemane, Jesus is determined to tread the path to Calvary (*see* vs 53,54). However, at a time in history when acts of extreme violence seem to be proliferating, we need to ask whether the Saviour's repudiation of the sword at this critical moment does not have implications for the shape of Christian living today.

Think about the question raised here: what does it mean to follow the Prince of Peace[4] in a violent world?

[1] Peter, according to John 18:10 [2] Matt 5:38–47 [3] M Hengel, *Victory over Violence*, Fortress Press, 1973, p58 [4] Isa 9:6

THE JUDGES JUDGED

Father, as we see Jesus accused, abandoned and alone, strengthen our resolve to stand with him, whatever the cost.

MATTHEW 26:57–68

The French artist Georges Rouault[1] painted some disturbing pictures of magistrates sitting in judgement on people who were poor and dispossessed. Rouault found the idea of human beings judging other people terrifying and wrote that all the riches in the world could never persuade him to take the position of a judge.

In this passage Jesus is placed on trial, and the full weight of legal authority and tradition is employed to find evidence that would result in a guilty verdict. And yet, despite the overwhelming power of the court (notice the statement that 'the whole Sanhedrin' was involved in the search for incriminating evidence, v 59), it is the accused who warns his interrogators of a greater assize still to come, so that the judges find themselves judged! At the climactic moment in this exchange, Jesus openly acknowledges his Messiahship, but makes it clear that he understands this, not in narrowly nationalist terms, but in relation to the mission he has undertaken, the life he has lived, and the death he is about to die as the 'Son of Man' (v 64).

With this, our studies in Matthew 24-26 come full circle. Remember that this section of the Gospel began with the enquiries of the disciples concerning the destruction of the temple and 'the end of the age' (24:1-3). Both these themes now reappear: Jesus' attitude towards the temple forms part of the charge against him (v 61), while he himself anticipates the end time when his life of suffering and obedience to the Father will be vindicated and he will be revealed as the one person worthy to act as the judge of all the earth. Before such a claim, only two responses are possible: either Christ is rejected, as tragically happens here (vs 65-68), or we confess him as Saviour and Lord and offer him all that we have and are.

Reflect on the radically different responses that Jesus provokes, and ask him to show you what walking in his way really means for you today.

---

[1] 1871–1958

RESPONDING TO PRESSURE

As we approach the end of this Gospel, let us meditate on the way of the cross, the path of dying and rising, and the road to eternal life.

MATTHEW 26:69–75

Matthew reveals the differing reactions of Jesus' friends to his ordeal: fear among the disciples, the devotion of the women, the courage of a secret follower. He writes most about Peter. No one in the early church would invent anything so embarrassing about their leader. Mentioned in every Gospel, surely Peter himself publicised his failure to encourage those who had similarly failed when facing persecution. Jesus' courage and Peter's cowardice are displayed simultaneously. Both faced three verbal threats – Jesus from false witnesses, true witnesses and Caiaphas, and Peter from two maids and some bystanders. Jesus responded bravely. Peter's denials escalated, denying knowledge of Jesus, swearing he didn't know him and finally distancing himself by cursing.

Many translations soften verse 74, having Peter curse himself. The original Greek says that Peter 'cursed and swore', implying that he called on God to punish him if what he said wasn't true. Matthew had already warned of coming persecution, urging his readers to stand firm under pressure,[1] which can only mean pressure to deny their Lord. Pliny, Roman governor of Bythinia, when judging people accused of being Christians, always tried to make them curse Jesus. In the Pacific during World War II, missionaries were martyred for refusing to dishonour Jesus. Still today people in difficult places are forced to conceal or deny their faith or face hardship and death. We in less hostile environments should not judge them, knowing how weakly we respond to far less threatening pressures. Peter's story is a warning and an encouragement. There is failure, but also forgiveness. John records Peter's reinstatement[2] but Matthew didn't need to. For Peter was among those whom, despite their doubts and failures, Jesus sent out to proclaim him to a sometimes hostile world.[3]

Pray for our fellow-believers facing persecution, that they may know Jesus' presence, giving courage as they face danger and possible death.

[1] Matt 10:21–22 [2] John 21:15–19 [3] Matt 28:16–20

THE AWFUL CHOICE

'O God, without you we are not able to please you: mercifully grant that your Holy Spirit may in all things direct and rule our hearts ...'[1]

MATTHEW 27:1–10

Matthew records that, overcome with guilt and remorse, Judas took his own life. Suicide is alarmingly common in the Western world, and the subject of much research. We now know much more about it. One undeniable fact is that its causes are not simple. Does Judas' remorse suggest that his 'betrayal' of Jesus was more complex than meets the eye? Yes, he was notoriously avaricious,[2] but did he act out of avarice alone? Did he callously want to profit from the execution of his leader, or did he imagine that Jesus would resist his arrest? Judas had seen Jesus calm the storm and raise the dead. Was he expecting the 'twelve legions of angels' to rescue Jesus?[3] If Judas misunderstood Jesus' mission, he was not alone among the disciples. As Jesus' arrest led inexorably to his execution, Judas regretted what he had done, but he still failed to comprehend. Instead he took the ultimate way out and killed himself. Among all the unanswerable questions Judas raises for me, the most difficult is how he could spend so long in the company of the Son of God and share in his ministry and yet be so completely wrong. He still did not understand that despite it all he could have thrown himself on the limitless mercy of the God of grace whom Jesus had proclaimed.

Why is the suicide rate so high today, especially among young people? Is it in part due to a failure of the church to witness powerfully to the grace and mercy of God? Preoccupied with its internal politics, publicly shamed by revelations of immorality and tainted by an uncritical acceptance of materialism, the church is becoming increasingly less effective in presenting to a desperate world a merciful God whose forgiveness has no bounds and who can 'save to the uttermost'.[4]

Does your church take seriously the emotional needs of modern youth? Would young people feel that your church would judge them, or try to help them?

[1] *A Prayer Book for Australia* [2] John 12:6 [3] Matt 26:53 [4] Heb 7:25, AV

MATTHEW AND THE JEWS

'God of the ages, you call the church to keep watch in the world and to discern the signs of the times: grant us the wisdom that your Spirit bestows ...'[1]

MATTHEW 27:11–26

'He ... suffered under Pontius Pilate.' I repeat this ancient formula weekly, affirming not only that Jesus suffered but that he was a real man whose life coincided with a Roman governor known to secular history. Has 1,700 years of reciting the creed predisposed us to blame Pilate for Jesus' death? Matthew clearly intends to teach otherwise, to absolve Pilate and blame the Jewish leadership. To Mark's terse account, Matthew adds Pilate's wife Procula's dream, his hand-washing, his denial of responsibility and the people's ominous acceptance of liability. Significantly, Matthew shifts focus from the anonymous 'crowd' (v 20) to the 'people' (v 25), the word he uses for Israel. God's chosen people assume the guilt of Jesus' death.

'No wonder you Christians hate the Jews!' The anger of my Jewish friend, a violinist recruited into our orchestra to perform the *St Matthew Passion*, surprised me. We had sung, 'Let his blood be on us and our children.' As a young man, I was discovering for the first time that Matthew's words could fuel anti-Semitism. Later I learned that many great figures in Christian history advocated the punishment of Jews, the 'Christ-killers'. Still today easily accessed websites promulgate the same hatred. But Matthew, who alone records Jesus' words, 'Blessed are the peacemakers',[2] was not promoting racism but expressing deep theological truths. That Israel rejected its Messiah is a crucial theme in his Gospel. Citizens refuse to repent; leaders plot Jesus' death; guests refuse the banquet; tenants are evicted from the vineyard; subjects lose the kingdom.[3] By the time Matthew wrote, Jerusalem was destroyed and the unstoppable gospel was loose in the world. The vineyard had new tenants. God's kingdom, characterised by love, was to be one in which there was neither Jew nor Gentile.[4]

On the cross, God puts to death human hostility.[5] How could the gospel message overcome racial or religious divisions in your community?

[1] *A Prayer Book for Australia* [2] Matt 5:9 [3] Matt 11:20; 12:14; 21:41; 22:5 [4] Gal 3:28; Col 3:11 [5] Eph 2:16

AMONG THE SCOFFERS?

'... O most merciful Friend, Brother and Redeemer; may I know you more clearly, love you more dearly, and follow you more nearly, day by day.'[1]

MATTHEW 27:27–44

'How deep the Father's love for us ...' With moving words and haunting melody, Stuart Townend's beautiful hymn is a favourite with our little suburban congregation.[2] Recently I sat pondering the second verse: 'Ashamed, I hear my mocking voice call out among the scoffers'. Is that where we would be? Giving few details of the crucifixion, Matthew concentrated on the spectators. With no nails, no blood, no pain, no thirst, little even of Jesus, Matthew hammered home his true but appalling point: Israel finally and absolutely rejected its own Messiah. Religious leaders taunted him. Passers-by ridiculed him. Fellow-sufferers insulted him. But not all mocked. Some mourned. Some were indifferent. Even Matthew noted the distant little group of distraught but faithful women[3] and the execution party, suppressing their aversion to an unpleasant job by gambling and drinking cheap grog. Other Gospels record the weeping 'daughters of Jerusalem'[4] and at least one disciple.[5] Then there were the absent ones. Most disciples had panicked and fled. In the governor's palace, Pilate and his wife knew what was happening. Ordinary folk went about their business. In both city and countryside, many knew nothing of it or, if they did, avoided it.

Looking around our church, named after Simon of Cyrene, I see many who also carry crosses that are hard to bear, not of their own choosing. Would we have been among the scoffers? We cannot know, but we are Jesus' followers now. Back then, some of us might have fled in confusion; a few of us might have stayed weeping near the cross. In the world outside, people still react to Jesus' death in the same ways, sometimes in sympathy, often in hostility, scorn, apathy or ignorance.

Lord Jesus, when people scoff or just don't care, help us to show them how deep the Father's love is by loving them as you did.

[1] Richard of Chichester, 1197–1253 [2] © 1995 Kingsway's Thankyou Music
[3] Matt 27:55 [4] Luke 23:28 [5] John 19:26

ENDING WITH A QUESTION

'I confess my iniquity; I am troubled by my sin.'[1] Father, your Son's cross makes me so aware of my sin. Thank you that it is also sin's remedy.

MATTHEW 27:45–56

'How great the pain of searing loss – the Father turns his face away.'[2] Did the Father forsake his Son? I was intrigued as a child with this paradox: 'If Jesus was God, how could he forsake himself?' Actually, this is no mere childish curiosity but a deep question, asked ever since Jesus died. We cannot explain the mystery of how Jesus was fully human and fully God but, in faith, we must believe it absolutely – heresies always arise from weakening this paradox, making Jesus less than God or not quite human. If Jesus was fully human there was no depth of physical pain, emotional loss or mental anguish he could not feel. To believe otherwise alleges that by being God, he was less than a man. Jesus felt abandoned, his last words an excruciating question, a scream of anguish but not of despair. Not lack of faith but faith leads someone to cry out to God.[3] Jesus screamed his question, not to an unfeeling universe, but to 'my God'. Jesus used David's cry,[4] so some commentators diminish Jesus' question, suggesting he was pointing to the triumphant note on which the Psalm ends. But Matthew did not suggest that, and the bystanders certainly understood it as a desperate cry for help. Jesus was the sinless Son of God. If God abandoned him, it could only be because he was 'giving his life as a ransom' for us all.[5] Separation from God is the price of sin,[6] the price that Jesus was paying.

The curtain was torn from the top, that is, God did it, his first and most powerful comment on the death of his Son. Jesus had died for the sins of the whole world. The system that denied Gentiles access to God was destroyed. The era of the new covenant had begun.

O God, sometimes you seem far away. We cry out to you in our darkness. Come to us and save us for the sake of Jesus Christ your Son.

---

[1] Ps 38:18 [2] Stuart Townend, © 1995 Kingsway's Thankyou Music [3] eg Ezek 11:13; Rev 6:10 [4] Ps 22:1 [5] See Matt 20:28 [6] Deut 31:17; Rom 6:23

DEAD AND BURIED?

'Today a tomb holds him who holds creation in the hollow of his hand; a stone covers him who covered the heavens with his glory.'[1]

MATTHEW 27:57–66

Harmonising the Gospel passion narratives is like doing a jigsaw with pieces missing. The writers had their own purposes, selecting their material carefully to stress their own message. Within a few decades of Jesus' death, they were concerned with questions relevant to their context, unaware that Jesus' resurrection would still be debated in the 21st century. In Matthew's time, none could doubt that after Jesus' crucifixion a vigorous movement emerged, based on the belief that he had risen from the dead. Then, as today, Jesus' death was controversial. Docetism was emerging, the view that a divine, non-human Jesus only appeared to die. In contrast, the many sceptics and opponents of Christianity wanted a human Jesus, dead and gone, his resurrection a myth created by his followers. Myths and literary inventions have always surrounded history's most significant figure, some of which Dan Brown cleverly manipulated in *The Da Vinci Code*, yet another deceptively convincing fabrication.

Matthew needed to show that Jesus really died. Otherwise he could not be raised from the dead. All four Gospel writers clearly assert that the real body of the real Jesus was placed in a recognisable tomb, not lost in an unmarked mass grave or a temporary location that might later be confused. Matthew also records the guard, countering the accusation of body theft. And there were known witnesses. The two Marys observed everything and the whole burial was organised by the enigmatic Joseph of Arimathea. Matthew invites us to contrast the cowardice of Peter, a known disciple, with the courage of a secret sympathiser. Legend sends Joseph to the quintessentially English site of Avalon, source of the medieval claim that he brought the Holy Grail with him, but he does not need Arthurian legend to make him heroic: when others failed, he set aside status and risked his future.

Lord Jesus, when others fail you, may we not fail. When others flee, help us to find the courage to be faithful to you.

1 Mattins, Holy Saturday (*Festal Menaion: The Servicebook of the Orthodox Church*)

HE HAS BEEN RAISED

'Love's redeeming work is done, fought the fight, the battle won ... Vain the stone, the watch, the seal; Christ has burst the gates of hell.'[1]

MATTHEW 28:1–10

The witnesses mattered to Matthew. The guards were useless, fainting at the crucial moment and later concealing the true facts.[2] In the real story of the real rising of the real Jesus there were only the women. The chief witness, named in all four Gospels, was the much maligned and much revered Mary Magdalene. From earliest times, her relationship to Jesus has been speculated upon. No evidence indicates she was a prostitute, we know only that Jesus healed her of terrifying demonisation, and that she left her previous life to follow him.[3] In *Jesus Christ Superstar*, she 'didn't know how to love him'. In *The Da Vinci Code*, she bears his child. Why are people eager to believe Dan Brown's fiction? Well, everybody loves a romance, especially a celebrity romance, and what greater person than Jesus! People are also intrigued by conspiracies, only too ready to believe a somewhat discredited church capable of a big cover-up. But at a deeper level, people want a Jesus who is only human, whose teachings about love and mercy they can admire, but not someone who is God.

Hundreds of Jesus' followers saw the risen Jesus,[4] but in Matthew's narrative only Mary Magdalene and 'the other Mary' were present at the exact moment. Imaginative writings like the second-century Gospel of Peter invent a grander scene with spectators, a talking cross and monstrous angels reaching from earth to heaven. But only two frightened women heard the radiant angel of the Lord announce that 'he has been raised' (v 6, NRSV). Jesus did not merely rise from the grave; God raised him.[5] That is the force of Matthew's powerful narrative, the issue that made other details irrelevant. Jesus really died, so that God alone could raise him to new life.

'Let us not mock God with metaphor, analogy, sidestepping transcendence, making of the event a parable, a sign painted in the credulity of earlier ages ...'[6]

---

[1] C Wesley, 1707–88, 'Christ the Lord is risen today' [2] Matt 28:11–15 [3] Luke 8:1–3 [4] 1 Cor 15:6 [5] Acts 2:24,32 [6] J Updike, 1932– , 'Seven Stanzas at Easter'

TO THE END OF THE AGE

'O God, you are my God, earnestly I seek you; my soul thirsts for you, my body longs for you, in a dry and weary land ...'[1]

MATTHEW 28:11–20

Matthew tells us of the reliable witnesses to Jesus' death and rising, but he knows that resurrection faith is not just a matter of evaluating evidence but rather of experiencing the reality of the risen Jesus. Faith is more than believing that the tomb was empty, that a dead body came back to life. The soldiers and the chief priests knew that, but knowledge and faith are not the same thing. Overcome with doubt and wonder, the disciples assembled in Galilee where it had all begun, perhaps at the actual site of the Sermon on the Mount. There Jesus came to them. What passed between them we cannot know, but surely Jesus stayed there for more than the ten seconds it takes to say Matthew's summary of what Jesus said.

Since William Carey in the 1790s, this 'great commission' has been 'the mandate for mission' for the Protestant missionary movement, and generations of missionaries have proclaimed the risen Jesus around the world. But in the words of the old Authorised Version it had an imperial tone, consistent with European colonial expansion: 'power ... go ... teach ... world.' In this rendering there was a risk of mission being seen as a burden to be carried rather than a joy to be shared, our programme rather than the Spirit's work. Modern translations are truer to Matthew's recollection: 'authority ... go ... make disciples ... age.' Through death and resurrection, God has exalted his Messiah to his 'right hand'.[2] Yes, we are to go, but Matthew emphasises not our preaching but its purpose, creating disciples with faith in the risen Jesus, who live the way he taught. And he will be with us, not just to the end of the world, but to the end of time; Matthew did not write 'always' but 'all the days'.

Lord Jesus, raised from death and alive for evermore, come to us this day as you came to your disciples of old and send us out to live the way you taught, through all our days.

---

[1] Ps 63:1, NIV [2] Ps 110:1; Rom 8:34

MARK

Mark is the shortest Gospel, compressed and concise. Full of action, the word 'immediately' hurries us on from one amazing story to the next.

Mark was the cousin of Barnabas (Colossians 4:10). He lived in Jerusalem with his mother, Mary (Acts 12:12), went with Paul on his first missionary journey (Acts 12:25; 13:5) and was close to Peter (1 Peter 5:13). It is generally accepted that Mark wrote down the good news as he heard it from Peter. It is possibly the earliest Gospel, written between AD 65 and AD 70 before the Jerusalem Temple was destroyed.

Mark is keen to show his readers that Jesus is the Son of God, but also the humanness of Jesus. Miracles point to his deity, but also to his compassion and kindness. Following the feeding of the four thousand and the healing of the blind man at Bethsaida, Jesus asks Peter: "'But what about you?" ... "Who do you say I am?" Peter answered, "You are the Messiah"' (Mark 8:29).

Outline

1 Prologue	1:1–13
2 To and fro in Galilee	1:14 – 7:23
3 Jesus in the north	7:24 – 9:50
4 The move south	10:1 – 13:37
5 The focus of all history	14:1 – 16:8
6 Epilogue	16:9–20

ALL ABOUT JESUS

'I bind unto myself today the strong name of the Trinity, by invocation of the same, the Three in One, and One in Three.'[1]

From first to last this passage is about Jesus. We are told who Jesus is (v 1) and what Jesus will do (v 8). Although when the curtain goes up the only actor on the stage is John, he appears here only as a witness. First he is identified as the promised forerunner (v 2), but the forerunner goes before the face of God himself.[2] If John is that forerunner, then Jesus is no mere prophet but the Son of God and his personal representative. Then John tells us that Jesus will usher in a new experience of the Spirit, which Mark's readers know to be their new life in Christ, in comparison to which John's own ministry can be seen as merely preparatory (vs 7,8).

Baptising with the Holy Spirit is not mentioned here as merely one of many things Jesus will do. It is chosen by Mark from all that John the Baptist said about Jesus as a summary statement that embraces all the benefits he has won for us. Jesus came to bring us into a new relationship with God: knowing God as our Father and knowing ourselves to be his children.[3] It includes both the forgiveness of sins and the promise of eternal life, and for this to be possible Jesus will have to die and be raised to life. Before the story proper begins, Mark tells us that this was the ultimate purpose of Jesus' living and dying.

Like John, evangelists and pastors today perform a task that is ancillary and preparatory to this ministry of Jesus. Word and sacrament do not bestow the Spirit, but they work to bring people to a new mind, which is what repentance means (v 4), and so prepare the way for Jesus to pour out the Holy Spirit into our lives.

Pray that God will give to his church evangelists, pastors and teachers who will discharge their ministry with humility and urgency. Should you be one of them?

---

1 'Patrick's Breastplate', translated by Cecil Frances Alexander, 1818–1895
2 Mal 3:1   3 Gal 4:6,7

JESUS, PROTOTYPE SON

'I bind this day to me for ever, by power of faith, Christ's incarnation, his baptism in the Jordan river, his death on cross for my salvation.'

MARK 1:9–13

Baptism has often been a subject of controversy among Christians. But we shall not go wrong if we see Jesus' baptism as the model and prototype of our own, as we surely may, remembering that Jesus is the 'pioneer' of our salvation[1] and that as Messiah he embodies and represents his people. We are 'baptised into Christ', and what is true of him is true of those who are in him.[2]

Jesus was baptised as an act of obedience. John's baptism, we recall, was a baptism of repentance. Jesus had no sins to repent of, but he could still turn to his Father and commit himself afresh to do his will. Turning from sin and turning to Christ in obedience should still find expression in our baptism. Jesus' baptism was followed by a moment of empowering. In Peter's summary of the gospel story, 'God anointed Jesus of Nazareth with the Holy Spirit and power', as a result of which, 'he went around doing good and healing all who were under the power of the devil, because God was with him'.[3] Those who commit themselves to do God's will are not left without the strength to carry it out. Jesus' baptism was followed by a word of assurance, and what God said to Jesus he says to us. He is the Son of God by nature and we are the children of God by adoption, but God still says to each of us, 'You are my own dear child and I am pleased with you.'

It has often been noted that God's word to Jesus echoes what he says to the Suffering Servant in Isaiah,[4] so it is no surprise to find that from the time of his baptism Jesus finds himself pitched into conflict with the power of evil.

Remember your own baptism, what God said to you and what you said to God (or what was said on your behalf). Which do you most need to remember today?

---

[1] Heb 2:10 [2] Gal 3:27 [3] Acts 10:38 [4] Isa 42:1

REGIME CHANGE

'His bursting from the spiced tomb, his riding up the heavenly way, his coming at the day of doom, I bind unto myself today.'

'Regime change' is an unlovely expression with bad vibes for some, but it is what people in many countries long for. Regime change is what is meant by the kingdom of God. It is a longed-for event (not a place or an ideal), the coming of God to overthrow corrupt rulers and the evil spiritual forces behind them, to put an end to suffering and to swallow up death itself in victory.[1] As such it is definitely 'good news' (v 14)!

Jesus fully shared his people's longing for regime change, even if he had different ideas of what it would look like and how it would come about. It will take the whole of Mark's Gospel to tease this out, but here at the start Mark summarises Jesus' preaching to make three things clear. First, the kingdom was indeed something promised, which God would bring about when 'the time' was right. Secondly, that time was now. The kingdom 'has come near' and would be put into effect (Mark will show us) through the death and resurrection of Jesus himself. Thirdly, the kingdom would require a whole new way of thinking ('repent') on the part of God's people, and would demand total commitment from them.

The demand of the kingdom is then graphically illustrated by the call of the first disciples. Again we notice three things. First, they are called into a personal relationship with Jesus, not simply devotion to a cause. Secondly, they are to place this relationship above all other sources of security or worth, in one case daily work, in the other family solidarity. Thirdly, they are called to be actively engaged in bringing other people to share in 'the suffering and kingdom and patient endurance that are ours in Jesus'.[2]

Spend time recalling in what terms Jesus' 'call' first came to you. How has your understanding of God and his purposes grown since then?

---

[1] Isa 25:7,8; 1 Cor 15:54 [2] Rev 1:9

HIS AUTHORITY AND OURS

'I bind unto myself today the power of God to hold and lead, his eye to watch, his might to stay, his ear to hearken to my need.'

MARK 1:21–28

'They went to Capernaum, and … Jesus went into the synagogue and began to teach' (v 21). Who is 'they'? The four disciples with Jesus, presumably. Telling the story, Peter will have said, 'We went to Capernaum', making it plain that what follows is eyewitness testimony.

What impressed itself on the disciples no less than the synagogue congregation was the authority of Jesus (vs 22,27), both in what he said and what he did. When he spoke he did not speak about God, like a clergyman giving a homily; he spoke directly from God, like the prophets of old. Confronted with a man 'who was possessed by an evil spirit', he set him free and commanded the evil spirit to leave.[1] It was spectacular. It caused amazement (Mark uses two strong words for this, vs 22,27), but amazement is not faith. Wonder soon turned to unease and unease to outright opposition, as the gospel of the kingdom threatened vested interests and long-held beliefs. The liberation of this demonised man may be seen as a sign of the kingdom, both of its gracious character and its imminent arrival, but in itself it was little more than a preliminary skirmish. Sterner tests lay ahead and Jesus would have to offer up his life on the cross before the power of Satan over Israel and the world could be broken.

In the south of England, where I live, we do not expect to encounter demons very much, any more than we currently expect to be persecuted for our faith. We are not 'on the front line', but we are linked by prayer with those who are and we know that whatever we may be called to face, we can do everything through him who gives us strength.[2] That is the message of this story.

To think about: should the church expect to act with an authority similar to that of Jesus? How? Why?

---

[1] *See also* Acts 10:38   [2] Phil 4:13

THE LONG AND SHORT OF IT

'The wisdom of my God to teach, his hand to guide, his shield to ward, the word of God to give me speech, his heavenly host to be my guard.'

No one knows how much Jesus prayed. We assume that he was brought up to say the Shema[1] and pray the eighteen benedictions twice a day, like other faithful Israelites, and we know that he went regularly to the synagogue.[2] On the other hand, he does not seem to have prayed general prayers 'for those in authority' or for 'doctors and nurses', and he is not recorded as having prayed with or for the sick. He simply healed them with a word. Of course it is not wrong to pray for a person who is ill, but the story of Peter's mother-in-law suggests how this should be done. 'They immediately told Jesus about her' (v 30). It was enough. By contrast, Jesus had hard words for those who supposed that God would be impressed by long prayers,[3] and the prayer he taught his disciples is notable for its brevity. On occasion, though, Jesus needed to pray at length, as he does here (v 35). Mark tells us of another occasion following the feeding of the five thousand.[4] Luke tells us that Jesus spent the night in prayer before choosing the twelve,[5] and his ministry is framed by his temptations in the desert and his agonised prayer in Gethsemane.

All these occasions were times of decision or temptation. In this passage we see Jesus facing the temptations that arise from his popularity. The whole town has gathered about his door. Not for the last time, Peter articulates the temptation to follow the path of quick success and easy rewards and protests at Jesus' seemingly perverse blindness to the opportunities of the moment.[6] But Jesus has spent time in prayer recovering a sense of God's purpose for him, and he moves on. His task is to announce the kingdom of God as widely as possible, not set up the Capernaum House of Healing.

When you pray at length, are you trying to find out God's will for you, or are you trying to persuade God to do what he otherwise might not?

---

[1] Deut 6:4–9; 11:13–21; Num 15:37–41   [2] Luke 4:16   [3] Matt 6:7   [4] Mark 6:46
[5] Luke 6:12   [6] *See also* Mark 8:32

UNWELCOME PUBLICITY

'Christ beside me, Christ to win me.'

MARK 1:40–45

This story comes as the climax of a series of healing stories that show Jesus' authority and compassion. 'If you are willing, you can …' (v 40) neatly expresses the authority Jesus was perceived to exercise, while reaching out his hand and touching the man with leprosy showed his compassion more eloquently than a thousand words. The story also introduces the Jewish authorities who will engage Jesus in controversy in the stories that follow, but in such a way as to show that this opposition was not of Jesus' making.

Yet the story is puzzling. Why is Jesus apparently so angry? Some ancient manuscripts actually say that Jesus was moved with anger rather than compassion (v 41), but we don't need to accept that reading to see that Jesus is far from gentle with the man. The words 'strong warning' inadequately translate a word expressive of fury, while 'sent him away' hardly captures the urgency of the original Greek (v 43). Then we are told that because of the unwelcome publicity Jesus was unable to enter a town openly but remained out in the desert, so we are surprised to find in the next verse that he is in Capernaum, and he moves freely about the villages for the rest of the Galilean ministry.

Both these difficulties disappear if we suppose this incident took place later in the ministry, and that Mark chose to include it here to add to his picture of Jesus' authority. John makes clear that before his final Passover Jesus went into hiding at a desert location in the south.[1] A sensational healing at this point would have presented a direct threat to Jesus' need to remain hidden until his time had come. Hence Jesus' 'strong warning' and the speed with which he gets rid of the man.

This story exemplifies the great exchange at the heart of our salvation. The outcast is brought back into the family, while Jesus takes his place outside the pale.

[1] John 11:54

ASSURANCE OF FORGIVENESS

'Christ to comfort and restore me.'

First we have the heart-warming story of the paralytic and his four friends with their stick-at-nothing faith, which ends with his marching off carrying his bed. In the middle of this comes the story of the grumpy scribes who need to learn that Jesus has authority to forgive sins without recourse to the elaborate requirements of the temple cult. The two stories come together in Jesus' teasing question, 'Which is easier ...?' The answer surely is, 'Neither'. Both are equally easy to say – and in fact they are two ways of saying the same thing. As fallen human beings we are subject to both sin and death, and Jesus has come to set us free from both.

Like Jesus' other mighty works, the healing of the paralysed man shows that through him there is forgiveness of sins. Today we have this assurance not merely because of the healing miracles but especially because of the greatest miracle of all, the resurrection of Jesus himself. The miracles may be seen as a foretaste of the resurrection, and the resurrection of Jesus as a pointer to the resurrection of all God's people. The church is now sent by the risen Christ to offer the forgiveness of sins in his name. The forgiveness of sins carries with it a promise that we shall in God's good time participate in the resurrection of all God's people, when death will be no more and all sickness and pain will be done away with.[1]

Stick-at-nothing faith is still occasionally rewarded with miracles of healing, but that is unusual. The church's task is not to promise miracles but to declare that the Son of Man still has authority on earth to forgive sins, with the promise that those whom he justifies he will also glorify.[2]

The Son of Man has authority on earth, ie here and now, not simply in heaven when we die. Where is this authority located today and how is it exercised?

---

[1] Rev 21:4 [2] Rom 8:30

SCANDALOUS GRACE

'Christ beneath me, Christ above me.'

MARK 2:13–17

When the nineteenth-century evangelist DL Moody was leaving America to tour Britain, a pious lady asked him, 'Are you going to preach to the miserable poor, Mr Moody?' Moody replied, 'Yes, and to the miserable rich!' Jesus surprises us! We are familiar with the idea that Jesus reached out to the poor and marginalised, the blind, the lame and those with leprosy. But Levi was not poor and marginalised. He had an income, a position and colleagues. He may have been unpopular, grasping and unpatriotic, but he was hardly an outcast. Yet Jesus called him, and the initiative lay with Jesus. He did not wait for the man to come to him crying, 'What must I do?' As with the paralytic in the previous passage, he made Levi an offer he had never dreamt of, but would be mad to refuse. It was an offer without strings. There is no suggestion that Levi was asked to repay his ill-gotten gains or offer a sacrifice to atone for his sins. No doubt those who joined Jesus' fellowship went on to lead better lives, but Jesus never made that a condition of sitting at his table.

The reality of God's forgiveness was made plain by the meal they all shared. Mark uses words that suggest a feast or celebratory meal, a familiar symbol for the coming kingdom of God. No wonder the Pharisees were shocked. Jesus was not just letting the side down. He was opening the kingdom of heaven to all believers, irrespective of what they had done and without preconditions. Eating together had a significance in Jesus' world that it has largely lost in ours. 'Sharing a meal was an offer of peace, trust, brotherhood and forgiveness.'[1] As such, it was not lightly entered into. The Lord's table still makes this offer and makes it as widely as did Jesus.

The Lord's table is for sinners, and encourages self-examination and repentance. How successfully does your church welcome sinners?

---

[1] J Jeremias, *Theology of the New Testament*, SCM, 1971, p115

TIME TO MOURN OR DANCE?

'Christ in quiet, Christ in danger.'

MARK 2:18–22

Fasting was a traditional response to a national crisis. Esther, Nehemiah and Daniel all fasted when the nation was facing calamity.[1] The Pharisees fasted twice a week to express their concern for the desolation of Israel.[2] But Jesus and his disciples did not fast. Jesus said the kingdom of God had drawn near. God was on the move, healing, forgiving, setting free. This was a time to rejoice, not to mourn. Fasting at a time like this would be as inappropriate as mourning at a wedding (v 19).

Then Mark adds another remark of Jesus that seems to move in the opposite direction (v 20). The 'bridegroom' is now Jesus himself. He foresees a time when he will be put to death. That really will be a time for all true Israelites to mourn for the nation that has rejected its true king. What does this say to us, reading Mark today? The bridegroom was taken away – but returned to life. Christ has died. Christ is risen. Christ will come again. So is he with us or not? Is this a time to mourn or a time to dance? What do you think?

The same point is made by the parable of the wineskins. The new wine of the kingdom cannot be contained in the wineskins of the old religion. We nod happily, because the old religion is not ours, but then we remember that Christian history is littered with examples of old wineskins unable to receive some new work of God. From the safety of posterity, we cheer the pioneers and reformers who broke the mould and burst the skins, but are we in danger of resisting God today? Conversely, is it possible that some of us have been too ready to label ourselves as new wine and dismiss those who disagreed with us as old skins?

How can we tell whether a new movement is a work of God? What tests would it have to meet?

---

[1] Esth 4:16; Neh 1:4; Dan 9:3 [2] Luke 18:12

THE MAKER'S INTENTION

'Christ in hearts of all that love me.'

MARK 2:23 – 3:6

A tradesman was recently prosecuted by his local council for smoking a cigarette in his own van. The van, they ruled, was a place of work, so smoking was against the law. There are parallels between this apparently mindless interpretation of the law and this story of the Pharisees in the cornfields (what were they doing there?), finding fault with the disciples for allegedly 'reaping' on the Sabbath.

The Sabbath was in origin a good gift of God, 'made for people' (v 27), but the 'tradition of the elders' (7:5) had turned it into a law specifying 39 categories of 'work', each in turn broken down into six subcategories. The results could be either petty or cruel, as the two stories before us make plain. The intention was to build a fence round the law to guard against any unintentional infringement, and the law itself was seen as a fence provided by God to keep his people distinct from the other nations. But the fence that kept the chosen people in became in time a barrier that kept everyone else out. Now Jesus has come as the Son of Man announcing the kingdom of God, in which actions will be judged right or wrong by whether they enrich human life and meet human need, and God, through his Spirit, will refine our understanding of what constitutes fullness of life and what it is that humans really need.

It is easy for us to sit in judgement on the Pharisees for what seems to us to be wilful blindness to the obvious. We forget that not so long ago evangelical Christians were behaving in very similar ways. I remember with shame announcing to the rest of the family after my conversion that I could no longer join them for tennis on Sunday. Fantastic witness! Where did I get that idea from?

In what ways might you use a day of rest to save life and do good to others?

RADICAL SUBVERSION

'I am making everything new!'[1] The new creation is under way, and what Jesus has started he will complete. This is the hope that sustains us.

MARK 3:7–19

Jesus was not simply enjoying an outing after communal worship, his withdrawal (v 7) represents a pivotal moment in his life and ministry. The ugly confrontation with the Pharisees in the synagogue (3:1–6), provoked by their idolatry of the Sabbath, symptomatic of the destructive quality of their spirituality, and their abject failure to see God at work in his Son, marked Jesus' last attempt to engage meaningfully with 'the institution that had been at the centre of Jewish religion and cultural life for hundreds of years'.[2]

Jesus' appointment of twelve apostles, the same in number as the original tribes of Israel, was a radical announcement that the creation of a renewed people of God[3] was under way. 'Jesus was intent upon fundamentally reshaping the people of God, and as that reshaping was impossible within the existing structures of Judaism, Jesus created new ones.'[4] Jesus' renaming of Simon demonstrated something fundamental about this new community of faith – the centrality of grace.

Simon was no Peter, at least not yet, and it would be some time before the trust Jesus was placing in him, and the re-creative and restorative forgiveness God kept pouring into his life, made Simon into the rock that Jesus could already see. How wonderful that we, too, can intimately know this transforming love, expressed so poignantly by the one-time slave-ship captain John Newton: 'I am not what I ought to be, I am not what I want to be. I am not what I hope to be in another world. But still I am not what I once used to be, and by the grace of God I am what I am.'[5]

Thank God for the forgiveness he continues to pour into you. Ask him to help you relate to others in a way that reflects his grace and imitates his love.

[1] Rev 21:5 [2] RJ Kernaghan, *Mark*, IVP, 2007, p74 [3] 1 Pet 2:9,10 [4] RJ Kernaghan, *Mark*, p79 [5] John Stott, *Calling Christian Leaders*, IVP, 2002, p23

DIVINE SANITY

What draws you to Jesus? Take a few minutes to reflect on this question.

MARK 3:20–35

Consider the crowd that pressed upon Jesus the minute he came home. Who were they, and what was their motivation? We know that many were driven to him by their own needs: the poor and the sick, the confused and the searching.[1] Others were probably just sightseers, attracted by the healings, exorcisms, and controversy. Then there was the sinister presence of the scribes, religious officials sent from Jerusalem, part of the conspiracy to destroy Jesus.[2] The tension and conflict that would end with Jesus' crucifixion was already palpable. Jesus' own family were so disturbed by his radical attack on the religious/political hierarchy that they worried about his sanity (v 21).

The intensity and significance of Jesus' conflict with the Jewish authorities explains the apparent callousness of Jesus' response to the anxiety of his mother and siblings. (There can be no question that Jesus loved them deeply. Even when in agony on the cross, one of his last acts was to ensure that his mother would be cared for.[3]) What was at stake here was something of absolute importance – the careful and deliberate establishment of a new community of faith, a relational community centred on Jesus and obedient to him. How wonderful that we are part of this global, forgiven, relational community of Jesus' companions, in all its wonderful diversity and richness. The vehemence of the scribes' rejection of Jesus forced them into the venomous, though clearly ridiculous, assertion that Jesus was a tool of Satan, thus committing the unforgiveable sin: 'To identify the work of God as the work of the devil is to blaspheme against the Holy Spirit; it is the ultimate blindness, the point from which there is no turning back.'[4] What a tragedy when a person develops such resistance to God's overtures as to become immune to them, and moves beyond the reach of the Holy Spirit.

Prayerfully, thankfully, consider both what you receive and what you can contribute to the extraordinary community of Jesus' friends.

[1] Mark 1:32–34; 6:34; Matt 4:23–25 [2] Mark 3:6 [3] John 19:26,27
[4] RJ Kernaghan, *Mark*, p83

LISTEN, LISTEN, LISTEN

Choosing to follow Jesus is not a one-off decision, but an ongoing determination, rewarding but costly. Prayerfully reflect on this reality.

MARK 4:1–12

This is arguably one of the most significant stories Jesus told, which is why it is inserted between two urgent instructions. 'Both the verbs listen and hear are in the imperative mode. They are not invitations or declarations. They are commands, and no other parable in this Gospel is framed at both ends with an order to listen.'[1] Jesus couldn't have made it more clear to his large audience that he was saying something of immense importance, yet he deliberately spoke in such a way as to veil his meaning. What was going on?

Jesus knew what lay ahead. He knew that his word and work would polarise and divide.[2] He knew that many who eagerly sought him now would fall away, some deeply discouraged or disenchanted, others disapproving or even hostile. An easy sign-up was the last thing he needed to offer – something often forgotten in our enthusiasm to 'sell' the gospel. Most of the scribes and Pharisees were incapable of listening to the Spirit – the cumulative effect of a lifetime of decisions, small and big. Jesus' reference to Isaiah[3] is a pronouncement of God's judgement on such people. But those who yearned to know and understand God, who had an inner sense that Jesus was somehow the key to this, were listening with heart, head and soul. Perhaps this story was designed for them. Without doubt this assessment of how God's word would be received was primarily intended for the inner core of disciples.

It is so important for us to listen and keep listening, but how do we do this? We can quarantine time to read the Bible, to pray and to meet with other disciples. But the essential precondition is humility, for it is this which enables us to recognise and welcome God's love.

Lord, help us to listen to the disturbing voice of the Spirit. May our lives be shaped by your agenda, and enriched by your companionship and that of your friends.

---

[1] RJ Kernaghan, *Mark*, p86 [2] Luke 12:49–53 [3] Isa 6:9,10

THE CHOICE IS OURS

'The church is not made up of spiritual giants; only broken men can lead others to the cross.'[1]

MARK 4:13–20

Jesus clearly felt an urgent need to ensure that his disciples understood this parable, which is why he provided a simple explanation for their ears alone. He was preparing them for hard times. Jesus needed these 12 very hopeful but fallible men to appreciate that his way was not a way of easy triumphs and quick gratification. It wasn't until the trial and crucifixion that they finally grasped this fundamental reality.

Through this parable Jesus was explaining what it means to hear God's word – *really* hear it. Fundamentally, to hear God's word is to choose, and keep on choosing, to keep walking in Jesus' footsteps. It is about radically altered priorities and values. It is about the transformation that begins with an encounter with Christ and continues under the influence of the Spirit. This is the hearing that Jesus was demanding of his disciples – 'the commitment of the entire person, a successful life in relationship to God'.[2] To really hear is to choose to love and obey Christ, for this is the prerequisite for communion with God.[3]

Not all of us can point to a specific time when we decided that it was Jesus we wanted to follow, but we all know that this is a choice that continues to confront us. Each of us also knows of former companions in Christ who have chosen to listen to alternative voices, voices which we, too, have heard, and which often begin their subversive campaign with the faintest of whispers. The pressures and counter-attractions identified in the parable are not unknown to us. Moreover, we experience times of deep confusion, disappointment and impatience with God, sometimes even despair. Jesus knows this, and continues to love and challenge us through such times.

Pray for someone who is struggling to be faithful to Christ. If that person is you, remember what Jesus has meant to you, and quietly listen for the Holy Spirit.

1 DJ Bosch, *A Spirituality of the Road*, Herald, 1979, p77 **2** L Schottroff, *The Parables of Jesus*, Augsburg Fortress, 2006, p68 **3** John 14:23,24

TAKE HEART

'In God's world ... the last word does not belong to vicious ideologies but rather to the One who tenderly holds our history in his hands.'[1]

MARK 4:21–34

At least once a day, and often more frequently, I pray the Lord's Prayer. I find considerable personal meaning in praying daily, 'Your kingdom come, your will be done on earth', for it expresses a deep yearning within my heart. Confronted over and over again by the suffering inflicted upon so many people because of humanity's inhumanity, I long for God's will to be done on earth. Acutely aware of my own shortcomings, I long to imitate God more closely in the way I love and relate to others.[2] I long to see an end to the environmental vandalism which, fuelled by greed and an idolatrous materialism, is doing unspeakable harm to God's creation.

Can you identify with these longings? If so, allow these parables of the kingdom (vs 26-29,30-34) to bring you hope and encouragement, for surely this was Jesus' intention in telling the disciples these stories. Many who had initially sought and followed Jesus became discouraged early in his ministry and turned away.[3] These two kingdom parables were intended to reassure the remaining disciples that 'the kingdom will continue to grow inexorably, though sometimes almost invisibly, and that at the end of the age the kingdom will come into all its fullness'.[4] The parable of the growing seed assures us that the establishment of God's rule on earth is fundamentally his doing not ours, even though, amazingly, we are called to be his co-workers in this staggering enterprise. The parable of the mustard seed tells us that no matter how unpromising that enterprise may sometimes seem, it will not be overwhelmed and its consummation is guaranteed. Take heart: what Jesus has begun he will complete. In our darkest moments of disenchantment, we can and must believe what seems unbelievable.

Praise God, the time is coming, is indeed on its way even now, when all weeping will be over and distress ended – replaced by joy and delight.[5]

[1] D Tutu, in *Hope in Troubled Times*, Baker, 2007 [2] Eph 5:1,2 [3] John 6:66
[4] C Blomberg, *Interpreting the Parables*, Apollos, 1990, p266 [5] Rev 21:1–4

WHO IS THIS MAN?

'May we know thee more clearly, love thee more dearly, and follow thee more nearly, day by day.'[1]

MARK 4:35–41

To say the disciples were on a steep learning curve does not begin to do justice to the situation. The men who boarded the boat with Jesus were clearly captivated by him, and they stayed with him when many of those who flocked around him later retreated from his disturbing teaching.[2] Yet, despite the privilege of private tutorials from Jesus about the nature of the kingdom of God (4:34), they were a long way from grasping the truth as to who Jesus was.

This episode on the lake resulted in a pivotal shift in the disciples' thinking and awareness. Until now they had wanted to remain close to this amazing man who taught with such authority, healed the sick and cast out demons. Now, having witnessed his power over wind and rain, they were overwhelmed by great terror and awe (v 41).[3] Before this miracle they had undoubtedly been inspired by Jesus, but they had had no reason to see him as anything more than a very special man, a man who, like any other, needed to sleep after a day's hard work (v 38). The quelling of the storm changed all that, but it would not be until after the resurrection that they would truly begin to comprehend the answer to their question, 'Who is this?'[4]

Jesus made it possible for his disciples to share a deep, mutual companionship with him, but it was beginning to dawn on them that he was so much more, and they were awestruck. Much later, one of them sought to explain who Jesus really was, how in Jesus 'the Word became flesh', how through Jesus 'all things were made', and 'in him was life'.[5] Authentic intimacy with God nurtures not only gratitude and joy in the presence of love, but also a deepening awe in the presence of the holy.

Who is this man? Meditate on who Jesus is: Word become flesh, Saviour, Lord, Bread of Life, Light of the world.

---

1 Richard of Chichester, 1197–1253 **2** John 6:66 **3** TNIV 'terrified'; NRSV 'great awe' **4** Luke 24:44–49 **5** John 1:14,3,4

TERROR IN THE TOMBS

'God is love, and all who live in love live in God ... Such love has no fear because perfect love expels all fear.'[1]

MARK 5:1–20

What unimaginable horror! Cast out by family and neighbours, this despairing 'victim of demonic malevolence'[2] is forced to seek shelter among the dead. Living without the comfort of human embrace, he is separated from his former community by walls of fear, ignorance, hostility and alienation. He is utterly alone except for a host of demons whose only intentions were evil. His ceaseless roaming and peaceless howling, day and night, bore testimony to their cruelty. Tortured beyond the limits of sanity, his bondage was complete.

What amazing liberation. He who once appeared to be Godforsaken was now God-transformed – the first non-Jew to experience the liberating power of Jesus. Finally, after who knows how many years of incomprehensible pain and captivity, his suffering was over. 'Freed now, the man could be still ... His uncontrollable restlessness gave way to repose, his delirium to deliberation, his madness to meditation. This is what freedom in Christ does to people.'[3] The restored man, long denied the warmth of human fellowship, was eager to join Jesus' small band of companions. Jesus had other plans.

He instructed the former demoniac to return to his family and old neighbourhood, and tell them what had happened. So he did, and more. He shared his experience in the ten townships that made up the region of Decapolis, and the people were amazed. These townships were centres of Greek and Roman culture, ie they were not Jewish. Jesus' intention was clear: the good news of liberation was for everyone, not just the Jews. His recruitment of a Samaritan evangelist further demonstrated this passion, despite the agitation it caused his disciples.[4] Previously stigmatised, now she joyfully and effectively shared her experience of Jesus.

Are there any in your church's neighbourhood you may be tempted to think are beyond the reach of the gospel? Name them in prayer, and wait on God.

---

[1] 1 John 4:16,18, NLT [2] W Hendriksen, *Mark*, BTT, 1975, p189 [3] Evelyn Miranda-Feliciano, *Unequal Worlds*, ISACC, 2000, p28 [4] John 4:27–42

WHO DO WE SEE?

'I was sick and you took care of me.'[1] Remember Jesus' radical identification with the 'least' in society.

MARK 5:21–34

I cannot adequately comprehend the misery the unnamed woman in this passage had to endure for 12 long years. I am a man - and an extraordinarily privileged one. I have three university degrees. I have never experienced unemployment. I'm supported by a loving wife and family, and a global network of friends. I've had good hospital treatment when I have needed it. I have so much opportunity and choice. My life experience could not be more different from that of this woman - or from that of so many women in our world today.

This passage reminds us of man's inhumanity to women. Would a society in which women were equal with men tolerate a practice which heaped shame and abuse on a woman already suffering the physical pain and constant discomfort caused by unchecked haemorrhaging, and even exploit it for financial gain (v 26)? Jesus allowed her needs to interrupt his mission to respond to the request of a man of considerably higher status. He could have let her healing go unnoticed, but instead deliberately drew attention to her. Ignoring the cultural and religious marginalising of women in her condition, he publicly affirmed her faith and added the blessing of peace to that of healing. It was a powerful and public demonstration of God's care for a person so easily dismissed as being of little account.

Whenever and wherever Christians have grasped the foundational biblical truth that every person is made in the image of God, it has stirred us into actions of justice and compassion. As it dawns on us that every person, no matter how insignificant in the world's eyes, is loved and valued by their Creator and our Saviour, our way of seeing those pushed to the margins of society is transformed. To follow Jesus is to become aware of the suffering woman in the crowd.

O Lord, help us to see each and every person in the way that you do.

---

[1] Matt 25:36, NRSV

DESPERATE LOVE

'I will consider all your works and meditate on all your mighty deeds. Your ways, God, are holy. What god is so great as our God?'[1]

MARK 5:35–43

I remember the day my own daughter was born as though it were yesterday. This new life, so precious, so vulnerable, so loved, changed me for ever, for she made me a father. A profound feeling of responsibility centred itself in my deepest being. I can't imagine anything that would tear at a parent's heart more than the sight of a sick daughter or son slowly dying. It is doubtful that anything less than this could have driven Jairus, an elder in the local synagogue, to seek Jesus.

As one of the synagogue's leaders, Jairus 'was invested in the system of holy places, rituals and traditions that formed the fabric of first-century Jewish life'[2] – a system that Jesus challenged at every turn. In front of Jairus, he touched and blessed a woman who, according to those rituals, was unclean, and who 'had made countless people unclean'[3] as she pushed through the crowd. The abruptness of those who came to tell Jairus his daughter had died may indicate disapproval of his decision to seek help from Jesus. Was Jairus able to believe, as Jesus urged (v 36)? It seems unlikely, given his astonishment at what happened (v 42). Jesus' action was not prescribed by the father's conviction or lack of it. How horrible when formulaic theology attaches blame for a child's lack of healing, or even death, to a parent's inadequate faith. What cruelty it is to burden grieving parents in this way, and what a betrayal of the compassion of Christ!

For nearly 20 years, a small group has met fortnightly in our home to pray and wrestle with issues of faith and life. One of our members died from cancer, though we prayed fervently for his healing. Another was close to death, but rallied in the very hours we gathered to pray for him. It's an unfathomable mystery.

We know we will die, and we know God loves us. Prayerfully reflect on these truths.

[1] Ps 77:12,13 [2] RJ Kernaghan, *Mark*, p111 [3] Kernaghan, *Mark*, p111

JESUS REJECTED

'Teach me, O God, not to torture myself, not to make a martyr out of myself through stifling reflection, but rather teach me to breathe deeply in faith.'[1]

MARK 6:1–6a

'He was amazed at their lack of faith' (v 6a). How sad and deeply disappointed Jesus must have been. He had not been in his home town since his family's attempts to restrain him (3:21), and must have hoped that there would be at least a few from his own community and family who would be among the first to fully recognise his authority. Initially it might have seemed promising. The invitation to teach in the synagogue could be interpreted as demonstrating 'a degree of goodwill, or at least the recognition that Jesus is now a person of significance',[2] and at first the congregation was impressed by what they heard. However, in no time at all this morphed into a hostility which, according to Luke, reached homicidal intensity.[3] Jesus was confronted by the ugly violence of a lynch mob of former neighbours ready to take the law into their own hands.

Why such extreme anger and rejection? In both Mark and Matthew's accounts,[4] the only explanation offered is that Jesus' audience simply couldn't reconcile his wisdom and deeds with the fact that they had known this tradesman since he was a child (v 3). But was it really just a matter of 'familiarity breeds contempt'? Probably not. The extra information Luke provides regarding the substance of Jesus' message that day provides vital clues. He tells us that not only did Jesus pre-empt their antagonism by predicting it, which would certainly have fanned the flames of their anger, but he further incensed them by articulating the truth that God sometimes found more willing hearts and ears outside Israel than within it. Jesus was not denying the special significance of Israel, but the gospel announced by Jesus would not be constrained by tribe, ethnicity or culture. God is God of all nations, and Jesus was in the business of reaching out to all people.

Faith that is fragile and flickering is sometimes the best we can offer to Jesus. Yet it is sufficient, thanks to his grace and love.

[1] S Kierkegaard, 1813–55 [2] RT France, *The Gospel of Mark*, NIGTC; Eerdmans, 2002, p242 [3] Luke 4:28,29 [4] Matt 13:54–58

BABY TALK

Think of a time when the Lord called you to do something completely beyond your experience or skill. Remind yourself of what happened, and your feelings about it.

MARK 6:6b–13

I think this is one of the most amazing passages in the Gospels. Our pattern – so much more sensible! – is to put people through a training course, and then send them out to be missionaries or ministers. Jesus' pattern is exactly the reverse: send them out to teach and preach before they know anything, so that they can discover about relying on the power of the kingdom. Then they will be ready to come back and learn something – maybe... How encouraging! God loves to use the ignorant, because then their knowledge can't get in the way. They can be simple in their trust. Fancy setting off with no provisions at all for their journey, equipped only with trust that God will provide for and protect them – even when they are rejected and need to move on (v 11). The disciples had just seen Jesus rejected at Nazareth: hardly an encouragement for launching out themselves! But in this simple, obedient faith they will go, regardless, announcing the presence of the kingdom of God[1] by the way they look and live, as well as by their words.

Here's a challenging question: how can we learn to trust God, like the disciples on that mission, when we're surrounded by material stuff that makes it unnecessary to trust him? Secure with our extra tunics and shoes, we can devote time to making sure that our theology is excellent, our churches fully resourced, our mission programmes staffed by the best people, and our training establishments turning out graduates properly trained for the job! But... that's not the way of Jesus. He could have put them through a degree course before sending them out, but he didn't. It's far more important to learn to trust God in practice, than to learn to polish your theology.

Imagine that you are John or Andrew, one of the twelve, receiving Jesus' commission in verses 7–12 . How do you feel? Turn your feelings into prayer.

1 Mark 1:15

A WICKED, WICKED WORLD

Think of a dreadful incident reported recently, arising from human wickedness or cruelty. Pray for the people involved, both victims and perpetrators.

MARK 6:14–29

It's fascinating to ask why Mark chooses to report Herod's reaction to Jesus now. Why does he attach to it the flashback story about the death of John the Baptist at Herod's birthday party? We forget the darkness of the world at our peril. This whole story is framed by the mission of the disciples (*see* v 30) and this seems to be the point: the world into which Jesus sends his disciples is not just a world in which prophets are beheaded because their message is unacceptable. Far worse, it is a world in which John was beheaded even though Herod 'liked to listen to him' (v 20). That's because it is a world in which political power is hugely significant, for good and for ill. A corrupt world, in which powerful men can get the women they want, a powerful woman's hatred can get away with awful injustice, and a young girl can manipulate her newly discovered power over men to terrible ends.

That's our world: the world which will soon murder Jesus, like John, even though people say such great things about him (vs 14–16); a world in which people can be drawn to the good news, and yet still reject it, even with regret; a topsy-turvy world in which even tyrants are victims of public opinion (v 26), power is abused, and truth and justice are murdered.

What's the hope for such a world? In the story of The Sorcerer's Apprentice, the magic broom, chopped up by the apprentice, becomes many brooms, all drawing water. Even as John the Baptist is cut down, many new little brooms are emerging, ready to exercise the powers of the kingdom and spread its message. It will always be so!

Was there a clear or hidden political element in the incident you thought of? Pray for the political leaders who come to your mind – for honesty, justice and compassion.

SHEPHERD AND SHEEP

What attracted people to Jesus? Make a list of possible factors. What was the most significant draw, do you think? What attracts you to him?

MARK 6:30–44

His availability may have been one factor in attracting people to Jesus: here was a rabbi who didn't keep aloof, but allowed all comers to crowd round, so that he had no time to eat (v 31)! But it wasn't his availability that drew them in this story: Jesus tried to get away, but the crowds ran after him. Nor was it his healing power: only the fit could undertake that high-speed hike. No, it was his teaching that drew them: 'he began teaching them many things' (v 34). Rich teaching, nourishment for the mind and the soul! People will travel for miles if someone seems to offer insight and answers to the big questions they're asking. Other things will attract, too, but good teaching and real wisdom are probably top of the list in most cultures.

This makes the feeding miracle all the more strange! These men didn't need it. In Mark 8:2 Jesus waits until day three before raising the issue of food for the crowds. Here the disciples raise it, but not because there's any real problem. So why does Jesus perform this amazing feeding?

He responds to the disciples in a way which pulls them out of the shadows, and makes them the main actors. He sets them the problem, gets them to find the resources, and puts them out front, organising the crowd into groups and distributing the bread and fish. Suddenly, instead of Jesus feeding the crowd with teaching, the disciples are doing it, literally. 'Bread' in the Old Testament was a symbol of God's Law, his teaching for his people.[1] So Jesus has engineered a wonderful symbol of what he wants his disciples to do, permanently: to feed the world with his Word.

How do you think Christians could offer wisdom which pulls crowds, today? Pray about this, and imagine what would pull your neighbours and friends.

[1] *See*, eg Deut 8:3; Isa 55:10,11

ALL AT SEA

Think of a time – maybe now! – when God seemed very distant and life was really tough. Remember the experience and what sustained you, and turn your thoughts into prayer.

MARK 6:45–56

The theme of Jesus thrusting his disciples into the front line continues. They've just risked huge embarrassment, setting out to feed 5,000 men from their own meagre supplies. Now, Jesus 'compels' them (literal reading, v 45) to climb into the boat at the end of the day (when they would probably rather have spent the night where they were) and row to Bethsaida, without him. Presumably he knew that a storm was coming, even if these experienced fishermen didn't!

Mark seems to enjoy the symbolic quality of these stories, because they picture the life of faith for us. The disciples are thrown into an impossible situation, where they either sink or row. When Jesus eventually turns up, things get worse – he seems to increase the horror and danger. But then the horror and danger turn out to be him in disguise, and rescue emerges all unexpectedly. Does this fit with your experience of him?

Here's an interesting question. If the disciples had 'understood about the loaves' (v 52), how would that have made a difference? They might have understood that the things we worry about are no problem for Jesus. He knows we'll be OK. The disciples might have 'twigged' the background to the loaves, and the storm, in Psalm 107, which pictures the Lord God feeding and sustaining Israel on the way home from exile – and in particular stilling the storms that threaten to swamp the travellers.[1] Maybe the disciples would have understood that it was more important for Jesus to be alone, praying to his Father, than holding their hands and letting them avoid the challenge of radical trust. Maybe I'll understand that, too, the next time I'm in a storm and wonder if I can cope! The simple, clear faith of the Galilean crowds (vs 53–56) – that's what I need.

So, what might God be saying to you through this? In what way is he calling you to radical trust, now?

[1] Ps 107:23–30

RULES RULE OK!

Rules give comfort to the insecure soul – no wonder they are so attractive. Ask a radical question: in what ways might your church be guilty of what is in verse 8?

MARK 7:1–13

The attraction of legalism is felt in every age and place. It's the attraction of security, of knowing where we stand, of being able to judge difficult situations easily, of knowing that we're OK because we know that God is the same as us! The Pharisees and scribes knew, without a doubt, that God took the same view of purity as they did. For God, as for them, it was vital that hands were washed before eating - not for hygiene, but to wash away ritual defilement before eating. So keen were they on maintaining purity - for God's sake - that the Pharisees sought to treat all food as if it were priestly food, derived from sacrifices and designed for consumption in the temple. What devotion! But only if they've rightly understood God.

Jesus thinks they have gravely mistaken God. In this devotion to the minutiae of ritual purity, their 'hearts' are miles from God, as Isaiah charged (vs 6,7, quoting Isaiah 29:13). So keen are they that oaths must be kept, absolutely, for God's sake,[1] that they make it impossible for children to care for their parents! Jesus may have a particular case in mind in verses 10-13: imagine that siblings Reuben, Anna and Jonathan, in a burst of youthful religious zeal, dedicate themselves and all they have as an 'offering' (corban) to the Lord. They now 'belong' to the Lord. Later on, when they want to support their aging parents, the scribes stop them, telling them that their oath to the Lord takes precedence and they can't give away anything, even to their parents.

We can sense Jesus' anger in verses 6-13 as he denounces this denial of the fourth commandment. The problem with interpreting life through rules is that, sooner or later, mercy flies out the window.

Can you think of contemporary examples of this kind of legalism? Do you feel like denouncing it, like Jesus? What would you say, to whom, and how? Will you?

---

[1] Num 30:1,2

POT CALLING KETTLE BLACK!

To accuse another is a great way of boosting your own sense of status. It happens all the time, perhaps especially in politics! Have you noticed a recent example?

MARK 7:14–23

In psychology the process described above is called 'projection'. We usually do it unconsciously. The idea is that I avoid recognising my own darker features (the bits of me I feel ashamed of, probably) by 'projecting' them outward, onto others, and then roundly condemning them! That way, I can deny the presence of these features in me and feel good about myself as I denounce them in others. If we become aware of this happening around us, we might talk about 'the pot calling the kettle black'! An intense interest in issues of purity, such as the scribes and Pharisees had, usually derives its energy from projection. Such people usually need others around them, who can be condemned as 'impure'. As the Pharisees looked - often with genuine thankfulness - at the impure lives around them, they were bolstered in their own sense of rightness.[1]

Bad religion and bad politics are almost always energised by projection. Jesus turns to the crowd (v 14) - knowing that they are more likely than the Pharisees to recognise this truth - and exposes the whole phenomenon. Rather than projecting impurity onto others, we need to recognise it in ourselves. His list in verses 21 and 22 is horrifying: he's not saying that we're all guilty of all these things, but that we can certainly recognise ourselves in this list, and that's where our attention needs to rest. We are already comprehensively polluted in our 'heart' (v 19), long before we come into contact with others. Is it right to avoid contact with people who might badly influence us, or our children, or our churches, or wider society? To what extent? When does such a fear become a way of avoiding seeing bad stuff already present in us? How can we defuse such projection so that we see ourselves and others clearly? (Some answers on the next page!)

These are vital questions. Give some time to meditating on them, and turn them into prayer as you reflect on them.

[1] *See* Luke 18:9–12

SHE KNEW SHE WAS BAD

Most of us feel shame somewhere within ourselves – sometimes buried very deep. What about you? Reflect on where, and how, you feel ashamed. Pray about it.

MARK 7:24–30

This is one of the most beautiful stories in the Gospels. It follows from the preceding passage: hotfoot from his dialogue with the Pharisees, those champions of purity, Jesus goes straight to an unclean region (v 24a), where he enters an unclean house (v 24b), in which he talks with an unclean woman (a Gentile, v 26), whose daughter has an unclean spirit (v 25). The Pharisees would have done none of these things, for fear of defiling themselves, but Jesus has just 'declared all foods clean' (v 19), and we now begin to see the wonderful consequences of that. If all foods are clean, then there are no longer impure places and people, either!

Readers often feel uncomfortable about Jesus' words in verse 27 (where he seems to call the woman a 'dog') until they realise that he has not suddenly become a Pharisee himself, but is discerning her heart and reflecting how she feels about herself. She knows she is 'unclean', from a Jewish perspective. She has the deep inner belief that goes with the label. But now, out of love for her daughter, she is not going to let herself be directed by the inner message that says 'keep away: you're unclean!' Jesus' beautiful response to her - delivered with such empathy and love - elicits her beautiful reply, which reveals not only her own deep sense of uncleanness (she accepts the designation 'dog') but also her passionate love for her daughter (v 28). Of course healing follows: and not just for the daughter, but for the mother also, I believe, as she discovers the wonderful grace of this Saviour, who has broken down the wall between Jews and Gentiles and reaches out to all in need, without discrimination. In his eyes, she is not unclean.

Put yourself in the place of this woman. What memories or feelings are touched? Bring especially to Jesus the part of you that feels you are a worthless 'dog'.

HEARING, REALLY HEARING

Lord, save me from the deafness caused by thinking that I know you, so that I only hear familiar things...

MARK 7:31–37

Mark's miracle stories usually have a second, symbolic meaning. Yes, they point to Jesus' wonderful power and mercy – but the question 'Why did Mark choose this story to tell at this point?' usually leads to deeper meanings. This is a case in point!

The deaf man needs to be able to hear, in order to be able to speak. The crowd is amazed: 'He even makes the deaf hear and the mute speak' (v 37). In Mark 4, we heard about the deafness of 'those on the outside', who hear the parables but can't understand them, in line with Isaiah's words.[1] Then Jesus told a series of parables about perception (4:21–34), issuing the appeal, 'If anyone has ears to hear, let them hear' (4:23). At first the disciples seem to be in a privileged position, with everything explained to them in private (4:33,34), but just recently we've heard that 'they had not understood about the loaves; their hearts were hardened' (6:52). Oh dear! In Isaiah 6:9,10, hard hearts go with blind eyes and deaf ears to describe a people who simply don't get it. The Pharisees don't get it, for sure – but what about the disciples? They've been remarkably silent. What do they think about the woman in the previous reading? If it's true that the heart is the source of all that defiles us,[2] then the disciples are no better than anyone else. They – and we – have all got impure, hardened hearts that will surely deafen our ears to the word of God, unless...

Unless the Son of God himself puts his fingers in our ears and says, 'Be opened!' (v 34). The restoration of this man's hearing (and speech) is a wonderful symbol of what the Lord can do to make the deaf hear and the mute speak in other ways, too.

Renew that prayer for hearing that goes beyond your present capacity. Pray for grace to tune in anew to the voice of the Lord!

---

[1] Mark 4:11,12; Isaiah 6:9,10 [2] Mark 7:21

A DEAFENING SILENCE

How can we combat spiritual blindness in ourselves? By definition, we're not aware of it! Make a list of steps you might take. How do you feel about it?

MARK 8:1–13

There's a silence all through this story about the reactions and thoughts of the disciples. Like last time (6:35-44), Jesus thrusts them into the front line, to organise the crowd and then set out to feed them with woefully inadequate supplies. Imagine approaching a crowd of 200 adults with a single chunk of bread – trusting that something will happen to make sense of the situation! Obedience they can manage all right, as when they went out on their mission (6:7-13), but will they understand about the loaves this time (6:52)? Or will their hearts still be 'hardened'?

The Pharisees illustrate blindness (vs 11,12). At least the disciples have seen the sign – they were in the middle of it – but the Pharisees demand a sign immediately after Jesus has performed this amazing feeding, as well as many other miracles. It's true, they would have to believe the testimony of others, but it seems that, when Jesus says that no sign will be given to this generation (v 12), he means 'no sign can be given to this generation'. They are simply incapable of seeing a sign, because something within them resists the sight. They demand one, but can't receive one. No wonder Jesus 'sighed deeply' (v 12).

The disciples have seen the sign – but have they understood it? That's the vital question (6:52). Put yourself in their shoes, and ask yourself the same question. What does this feeding signify? How do you understand it? Make a list of possible meanings. If you can, compare notes with a friend. Did you make the same list? What motivated you, as you chose different meanings for the sign? How can you know whether they are right or not? How can we be saved from our blindness, from our incapacity to see Jesus clearly?

We end today with uncertainty – because that's where this passage ends. What does that feel like? Turn your feelings into prayer.

OPEN TO QUESTION

The first 'answer' to the problem of spiritual blindness is to be ready to be questioned deeply about our current understanding. Are you up for that?

MARK 8:14–21

In the UK Parliament, 'Prime Minister's Questions' is a weekly slot when the prime minister can be asked anything to do with government policy. 'Questions' and 'answers' in this setting are really 'attacks' and 'counter-attacks'! The earth would truly quake if the PM replied, 'Hmm, that's a good question. I must go away and think about that!' How would you feel, if someone questioned you as Jesus questions his disciples here? Would you jump to defend yourself?

The disciples are failing to 'see' something, signalled by their anxiety that they don't have enough bread. They've just seen Jesus multiply the stuff – but they can't expect him to do that every day, can they? And just for them, rather than for a huge crowd? So isn't it reasonable to think that normal life has resumed? What are they failing to see and understand? Jesus warns them against the 'yeast' of the Pharisees and Herod. The Pharisees are those who hear God's word and make it void because their tradition is so strong.[1] Herod is the one who hears God's word and rejects it because he cares more for good public opinion.[2] Both of them illustrate types of soil.[3] How can the disciples be 'good soil' now?

Look ahead to the next two stories. First a two-stage healing of a blind man: Jesus restores first his sight (8:23,24), and then his perception (8:25). What a wonderful picture of what needs to happen to the disciples! After that, the penny drops with Peter: 'You are the Messiah,' he says (8:29) – though it's only a small penny, because he doesn't understand about the cross (8:31-33). We grow in understanding with difficulty, and by degrees. The key to it is absolute openness to change, to have our perceptions remodelled by the Master Sculptor!

Turn these thoughts into serious prayer, that the Lord will reshape your understanding in whatever way he wants, at whatever cost.

[1] Mark 7:13　[2] Mark 6:20,26　[3] Mark 4:14–19

THE POWER OF TOUCH

'The world needs more words made flesh. The world needs more people to live the good news incarnationally, in a way that can been seen, heard and handled.'[1]

MARK 8:22–26

Mark is a documenter of detail, the Gospel writer who most gives us a visual close-up of the ministry of Jesus. With this healing, his reporting centres on touch. It is the touch of Jesus that these friends seek for their blind companion (v 22). It is by touch that healing comes: Jesus leads him by touch (v 23a), ministers to him by touch (v 23b) and then completes the healing, again by touch (v 25).

This matters for two reasons. To the blind man it matters because touch is all he has. He relies on touch to find security in his environment. Jesus knows this. To take his hand is to initiate a relationship of trust. Healing is administered in terms this man can grasp and understand. Jesus enters his world. To Mark, touch matters because he wants us to see the process by which healing is achieved. Real hands are involved, and real spit. Healing happens in the physical, observable realm of the body.

Mark is telling the story of the incarnation. The eternal God moves from the disembodied realm of the Spirit into our flesh-and-blood reality, so we need to know just how 'real' and physical these acts of healing are. Mark situates Jesus in the real world – setting the jewels of his teaching and miracles in the context of everyday reality. This is why he also shows us that the healing is not instant. Like a doctor asking if the pain has gone, Jesus checks with his patient after the first touch, to find that sight has only partly returned. It is the second touch that completes the healing. Physical effort is involved: real touch, and the passage of real time. This is a powerful portrait of how miracles happen and an important corrective to our desires for instant change.

'God of incarnation, come to our material world today. Teach and help. Touch and heal. Let miracles fill the streets you walk.'[2]

---

[1] J Hayes, cited by T Sine, http://msainfo.org/articles/the-new-conspirators-new-monasticism [2] www.twitter.com/twitturgies 22 December 2009

MOOD-SWING MESSIAH

'The incarnation involves an exchange ... God becomes one of us, even to the extent that he accepts suffering and death.'[1]

MARK 8:27 – 9:1

Mark's Gospel leaps from scene to scene with dizzying intensity. Having laid out account after account of healings and miracles, interspersed with significant sound bites of teaching, Mark now invites us to eavesdrop on a conversation between Jesus and his closest disciples. This is a dialogue of surprises. It begins with Peter, on behalf of the twelve, affirming that Jesus is indeed the Messiah (v 29). How could he not be, with healings, resurrections, mass feedings and profound parables so prominent in recent memory? Jesus then makes a leap in logic and begins to speak of his own future suffering and death (v 31). Peter, quick to speak and slow to understand, steps in – only to receive an almost violent rebuke (v 33). As Peter retreats to lick his wounds, Jesus goes on to explain that the way to life leads through the way of death (v 35).

Nothing is wasted in Mark's writings, and this dialogue serves a very significant purpose. It affirms with great clarity the linking of the miracles of Jesus to his sufferings. The key to understanding Christ's miracles is incarnation – we need to know that God has come in the flesh. This is also the key to his sufferings. God comes to us not only to take on our nature, but in his sufferings to redeem us: 'the incarnation of divine love in a world of sin leads to the cross.'[2] The death of Jesus is not an interruption of his mission, but its climax. This was a lesson it took Peter a long time to learn, and it became the cornerstone belief of the New Testament church he would later lead. Christmas and Easter are two chapters in one story. The Christ we welcome in incarnation is the Christ who gives his life for us.

'Incarnation is God's decision to dive into the ocean of humanity, even at the risk of drowning. May I learn to dare such love.'[3]

---

[1] G Arbuckle, *Grieving for Change*, G Chapman, 1991 [2] M Volf, *Exclusion and Embrace*, Abingdon, 1996 [3] www.twitter.com/twitturgies 10 December 2009

LOVE IS LISTENING

'Christians, especially ministers, so often think they must always contribute something when they are in the company of others ... They forget that listening can be a greater service than speaking.'[1]

MARK 9:2–13

Peter is widely believed to be a key source for Mark's Gospel. Details in the account seem to suggest that it is often his story that we are reading. It is significant, then, that there is such honesty in the telling of this tale. No detail is left out - even if to have done so might have saved face for Peter. In this story, Jesus gives to Peter, James and John the honour of joining him on a mountain retreat. In the course of this, a remarkable vision unfolds. Jesus is transformed before their eyes until he glows with heavenly glory, and Moses and Elijah - the two most powerful heroes in Hebrew history – appear to be in conversation with him. History and heaven come together in an experience that is deeply Jewish and at the same time profoundly new.

Peter's response is shot through with frailty and foolishness. First, he declares that 'it is good for us to be here' (v 5a), making himself and his companions central to an experience to which they are in reality only peripheral. Clearly Jesus wanted them with him, but the transfiguration is not about them - it is about him. Secondly, Peter suggests making permanent what is intended as a passing experience (v 5b). The building of booths is a traditional religious response to sacred experience: an attempt to fix the event in space and time; to create ritual around it. It emphasises the form rather than the content. The purpose of this vision, however, is that God might speak - affirming beyond doubt the divine mission of Jesus (v 7). Peter was not supposed to be talking, or building, or suggesting. He was supposed to be listening. He is the 'everyman' of Mark's Gospel, the typical and representative human. How often are we to be found talking and suggesting, when the intention is that we should listen?

'From every detour and distraction I am dazzled by, disentangle me. Every wrong turn redeem. Patient Father, prod me homewards.'[2]

---

1 Dietrich Bonhoeffer, *Life Together*, SCM, 1954 **2** www.twitter.com/twitturgies
25 October 2009

UNBELIEVERS ANONYMOUS

'We grapple with God in prayer until we have cast our burden on him. Then the burden is handed over to God. We are released from its power.'[1]

MARK 9:14–29

Jesus comes down from the mountain still glowing, it seems, with some echo of the transfiguration glory: the crowd who first see him are 'overwhelmed with wonder' (v 15). But he walks right into a dispute. The disciples left waiting for him have become embroiled in an argument with the Jewish scholars who have been following Jesus like a press pack searching for controversy (v 16). The argument concerns a boy who is demon-possessed, and whose deliverance the disciples simply could not achieve (vs 17,18).

The boy's father explains his condition to Jesus, who delivers the boy of that which has been tormenting him (vs 25–27). In the course of this, Mark is able to record one of the most powerful prayers found anywhere in Scripture – 'I do believe; help me overcome my unbelief!' (v 24). The simple faith of this father, desperate for his son to be well, is contrasted with the cynicism of the religious leaders (v 19), and the impotence of the disciples (vs 28,29). In a discourse that centres on belief and unbelief, the father is honoured not only for confessing his faith, but also for acknowledging the lack of it. Belief and unbelief are at war in him, just as they are both in the Jewish leaders and in the disciples – but he does something with this inner battle that neither of the other two groups do: he turns it to prayer.

The disciples' error is not that they lacked faith – it is that they were drawn into controversy instead of into prayer. Had they redirected their energies away from argument with the Jewish leaders and towards prayer, who knows what might have happened? Our doubts are not the enemies of the miracles of God, if we turn them into fuel for prayer.

'When doubts dig deep, may I yet say, "Lord, I do believe". When cynicism cuts to the heart may I cry, "Help thou mine unbelief".'[2]

[1] Ajith Fernando, *An Authentic Servant*, IFES/OMF International, 2006
[2] www.twitter.com/twitturgies 18 December 2009

PEOPLE POWER

'What our Lord left behind him was not a book ... nor a rule of life, but a visible community ... He committed the entire work of salvation to that community.'[1]

MARK 9:30–41

Great stories are driven by mystery. A question asked or a puzzle posed at the outset of a novel can keep the reader turning over the pages. How will it turn out? Who is guilty? We read on because we need to know. For Mark, one of the central questions driving the narrative is 'Will they make it?', the 'they' in question being the disciples. Jesus has just three years to prepare them, and at the end of that short time he will hand over to them, and to them only, the onward progress of his ministry. Peter has emerged early as leader, but he, too, gives cause for questions. Will he be a safe pair of hands by the time Jesus must pass the church on to him? Mark wants us to know that Jesus was intentional and focused in finding time to spend with his disciples (vs 30,31), but he also wants us to see that all was not easy. Even when Jesus took time to explain, the disciples were confused and afraid (v 32). Jesus' model of self-emptying leadership is new and revolutionary, turning upside down the preconceptions and assumptions of Jewish and Roman cultures (v 35). The journey from Galilee to Golgotha is a journey of learning and discovery for the disciples.

The fact is that when it really mattered they understood: on the day of Pentecost Peter was able to explain to others, so eloquently and passionately, what the new revolution was about – a testament to the effectiveness of Jesus' teaching methods. Lessons that seemed strange at the time – the welcoming of a child as a model of leadership (vs 36,37), a simple cup of water as an illustration of mission (v 41) – would later be remembered and passed on to thousands. Jesus was the ultimate investor in people.

'The ways of God are winding, but the working destination never wavers. For my good God goads me and into goodness I am guided.'[2]

---

[1] Lesslie Newbigin, *The Household of God*, SCM, 1955 [2] www.twitter.com/ twitturgies 21 September 2009

READY SALTED

'Prophetic voices are those which read the signs of the times ... and speak out against all that distorts or diminishes the image of God in human beings.'[1]

MARK 9:42–50

One very attractive aspect of Mark's Gospel is that it has not been sanitised or censored. When Jesus says things that are strange or confusing, or hard to hear, Mark does not hide them. So with the language used here. From forced drownings (v 42), via mutilations and amputations (vs 43–47) to the unquenchable fires of hell (v 48), Jesus uses graphic and disturbing imagery to make his point. We could have forgiven Mark for leaving out such teachings, difficult as they are to square with the Prince of Peace who will not break a bruised reed or snuff out a smouldering wick,[2] but Mark wants us to hear the full breadth of Jesus' teachings. He believes that these words are important, and because he deliberately passes them on to us, we can believe it too.

What is happening here? The clue comes in verse 50, where Jesus speaks of salt that 'loses its saltiness'. What does it take, we wonder, for a human life truly to reflect the character of God? How can we aspire to the life of goodness, truth and love that God calls us to? The answer is that we must face up to the laziness and narcissism that corrupts our every effort. We must be willing to do to death those aspects of our selves that are destructive to our own lives and those of others. Jesus, incarnate God, has come to show what an obedient human life looks like. He is our supreme example. His intention is not to soldier on alone but to empower us to walk with him: to renew in us the flavours of God. He is so determined to make us salty once more that he will resist in us every tendency and habit, every action and attitude, that twists our souls and distorts the image of the Father.

Strengthen me, God, to wrestle with the things you wrestle with. Do to death in me all that distorts and destroys. Salt my soul until I salt your world.

[1] Kathy Galloway, 'Singing the Lord's Song', in *Worship for Housing Estate Ministry*, National Estate Churches Network, 2003, p7 [2] Isa 42:3

THE LAW BENEATH THE LAW

'The people of God are called to scatter and mix, to mingle and move, to influence from a position of weakness, like a small child in a large family.'[1]

MARK 10:1–16

Note that there is no love in the question that the Pharisees asked (v 2). Like all legalists and fundamentalists, the Pharisees are not asking out of pastoral concern or human compassion – they are looking to score points; to trap Jesus, perhaps; to win an argument. Jesus draws attention to the poverty of their religion by pointing to the hardness of their hearts (v 5). The Laws of Moses are not the perfect reflection of God's will, he suggests, but temporary rules set up because our hearts are not ready for love. There is the Law, and there is the law beneath the Law. The Law speaks of behaviour; it codifies and clarifies. The law beneath the Law speaks of the heart. It sees intention; it honours humility and meekness. The law beneath the Law is love, and it is love that Jesus has come to show us. He does not abolish the Laws of Moses, but shows rather their intention. Jesus contrasts the issue of divorce – essentially a legal question – with the much more important issue of adultery – a question of the heart (v 11). It is what is happening in your heart that God most cares about. This is not a lower standard, but a much higher one, offering far fewer loopholes than the Pharisees had already found in the Laws of Moses.

As if to offer a visual model of the heart obedience he is speaking of, Jesus embraces and blesses the children others have brought to him (v 14). The faith of a child – unsophisticated, trusting, looking not for loopholes but for love – is the model God has always been looking for (v 15). The Law was a step on a journey. The destination is love. Weakness; vulnerability; simplicity of trust – let this be our model of faith.

'If I've been looking for loopholes, God, may I look for love. If I am a lawyer approaching the bench, may I be a child in a father's embrace.'[2]

---

[1] Pete Greig and Dave Roberts, *Red Moon Rising: The Story of 24-7 Prayer*, Survivor, 2003, p230 [2] www.twitter.com/twitturgies 23 December 2009

RICH, RELIGIOUS, RESTLESS

'The soul must long for God in order to be set aflame by God's love; but if the soul cannot yet feel this longing, then it must long for the longing.'[1]

MARK 10:17–31

From time to time a few words will capture truths of breathtaking importance. The shortest New Testament verse – John's unadorned 'Jesus wept'[2] – is one example, but Mark here offers us another: Jesus' reaction to the rich young ruler. 'Jesus looked at him,' he tells us, 'and loved him' (v 21). Jesus sees in this young man that from birth he has tried to please God (v 20). Jesus is not afraid to let his love for this stranger be apparent – noted by the eyewitnesses to the conversation. Having previously berated the Pharisees for their loveless understanding of God's Law, Jesus treats this young man differently because he sees the intentions of his heart. He honours the honest effort of a rich, religious young man to seek God.

So why does he challenge him with the impossible task of giving everything away (v 21)? Why make discipleship so hard? The answer is that Jesus is not demanding something of this man: he is offering something. For all the treasure he owns, he has not had the pleasure – the overwhelming joy – of self-emptying. What do you give to the man who has everything? The opportunity to have nothing. To make such an offer is to honour this man's spiritual journey – Jesus offers him the one thing he lacks because he believes him to be ready. And the offer comes with a prize – the opportunity to become one of Jesus' disciples.

Mark does not bring this story to a conclusion. We know that the young man goes away pondering Jesus' offer, struggling with its life-changing implications, but we do not know whether he made the change. God may show you a chapter in someone else's story – he may not choose to show you the end.

God, give me compassion for the spiritual longings of others. Open my eyes to honest intention, and my ears to a humble prayer. Those I look at, may I love.

---

1 Meister Eckhart, cited in Philip Yancey, *Reaching for the Invisible God: What Can We Expect to Find?*, Zondervan, 2000, p208 **2** John 11:35

A NEW WORLD IS COMING

'In the Gospels, we are presented with a perspective on power so radical and disturbing that few have understood or come to terms with it even today.'[1]

MARK 10:32–45

Mark works hard to set the scene for each important conversation he records. He works visually, wanting us to catch the story by picturing it. Here he lets us know that the plot is taking a turn – towards Jerusalem (v 32). Jesus, who knows why he is going there and the fate that awaits him, leads the way. Close behind him are the disciples, who are described as 'astonished'. They have been confused by the new, darker strand to Jesus' words to them, speaking of his own suffering and death, but hardly have they had time to ponder this when he sets off, heading resolutely towards confrontation with the Jewish and Roman authorities. They talk animatedly about what Jesus means to achieve. Somewhere behind them in Mark's picture is a larger crowd – also confused; also following where Jesus leads, afraid of what is about to happen. There is tension in the air. A cloud of dust rises from the feet of the growing crowd. Only Jesus knows the plan.

Seeing the confusion of the disciples, Jesus explains as plainly as possible the confrontation he is heading towards (v 33) and how it will end (v 34). But even this stark description is not plain enough for the disciples – they misunderstand completely, believing that a new government is about to be declared in Israel. They even begin discussing amongst themselves who should serve in Jesus' cabinet (v 37). 'Wrong question,' Jesus says (*see* v 38). 'Wrong understanding of power and leadership' (*see* vs 42–45). There is a revolution about to happen in Jerusalem. There is a change coming, a new kingdom, but it will not be like anything you have seen before (v 43). The fight is not for a new government – it is for a new world (v 45).

Empower me to understand, God, the workings of your kingdom. May I know what power is. What leadership means. What love longs for. What love will die for.

---

[1] Alan Storkey, *Jesus and Politics: Confronting the Powers*, Revell, 2005

SPONTANEOUS COMBUSTION

'I often hear Christian leaders tell what God has been saying to them … profound, eloquent things. All I seem to ever hear is: "Rob, get out of my way".'[1]

MARK 10:46–52

The kingdom of God is breaking out around Jesus. The crowd heading to Jerusalem has grown, picking up people as it moves. It has crossed the city of Jericho, creating a buzz of gossip and rumour. A blind beggar – well known in the city and to travellers passing through it – hears the commotion of the crowd. He catches snippets of explanation – 'Jesus of Nazareth, the prophet, is passing through'. Something stirs in his heart. Hope grows in him. Courage breaks the surface. He calls out to Jesus, 'Mercy!' Spontaneous and unplanned, the miracles of God combust where Jesus passes. Through three different reactions, Mark offers us insight into the workings of the kingdom.

First, there is Bartimaeus himself. Just as Jesus predicted at the outset of his ministry, the poor are hearing the good news. In the midst of crowd and noise and tension and movement this man, trapped in the horrors of darkness and poverty, hears the rumour of Jesus and cries out. The kingdom comes to those who are listening for it – those who have ears to hear. Others in the crowd are less sensitive. They try to silence the inconvenient beggar, to press him back to the margins. Not every ear is open to the coming kingdom. Not every heart understands. Some just get in the way of what God is doing.

Finally, it is the reaction of Jesus that most exemplifies the kingdom. He stops. He gives attention to Bartimaeus. He is purposefully heading towards Jerusalem, a great crowd following him. He has plenty to be dealing with, but he allows the blind man to come to him and asks him what he wants. A miracle ensues. Time, attention, love and healing: these are the gifts of which the kingdom is made.

'Into the broad and layered grace of God I sink. Into his great mercy I am folded. I trust. I let go. There is no risk in such a fall.'[2]

[1] Rob Bell, cited in R Webber, *The Younger Evangelicals*, Baker, 2002, p145
[2] www.twitter.com/twitturgies 7 March 2009

THE DIVINE IMPERATIVE

'I rejoiced with those who said to me, "Let us go to the house of the LORD."'[1]

'Almost there!' The air of expectancy was growing as the disciples approached the ridge near Bethphage, from which they would catch their first glimpse of Jerusalem. Their excitement would be intensified by contact with the thousands of other Passover pilgrims, as well as by their own memories. Personal memories of the annual family visits they had made since childhood; but also national memories – the stirring story of how God had delivered them from Egypt and formed them into a nation. It was these memories which made the authorities anxious – for they created an explosive atmosphere as people looked for a new national deliverer! For the disciples this year would have been extra special. In Jericho, Jesus had accepted the public acclaim of the blind man, 'Son of David'.[2] Was this the year that Jesus was going public on who he really was,[3] they might have wondered, conveniently forgetting what Jesus said would follow?[4]

The dramatic episode of Jesus riding into Jerusalem as King brings out for us three crucial aspects of our discipleship. First, we note that the disciples responded in obedience, when he told them to go and fetch 'a colt'. They might have been missing the excitement of being with the crowd, but they put service to Jesus above this, even though it was a somewhat puzzling request. Secondly, the willingness of the owner of the animal to allow Jesus to use it reminds us that discipleship requires the total surrender of all our possessions, not only our means of transport (whether car or bike) but everything from our home to our handkerchief! Finally, the disciples demonstrate truths about worship. Their adulation of Jesus was a response to who they understood him to be; a mixture of tradition and spontaneity, both exuberantly personal and very public.

Focus on one of the three aspects of discipleship above, prayerfully reviewing any ways in which you 'draw the line' or resist.

[1] Ps 122:1 [2] Mark 10:47 [3] *See* Mark 8:27–30 [4] Mark 8:31–38

THE DIVINE INITIATIVE

'Lord, you have been our dwelling-place.'[1]

MARK 11:12–26

Jesus here confronts the commercialism and corruption involved in changing money from 'secular' to 'religious' coinage and the insistence that only animals bought in the temple precinct were 'perfect' for sacrifice. It has been noted that in so doing he was signing his own death warrant, initiating his own death and therefore the atonement. Here is displayed what we read in John's Gospel: 'No one takes [my life] from me'.[2] There is more to it than that, however.

The quotation from Isaiah 56:7 is vital here. God wanted his temple to provide supportive access to him for all people, whatever their nationality. This distracting activity was taking place in the Court of the Gentiles, the outer circle of the holy place, so it meant that the Gentiles were robbed of their primary opportunity for encountering the God of Israel. The whole sacrificial system that God had initiated to enable people to renew their relationship with him had become a blockage. God's access route had been turned into a barrier.

Jesus, in ending the blockage, was symbolising what his death and resurrection would achieve permanently. This requires us to examine every aspect of our worship. Have rituals and procedures that were intended to help people find God now become a barrier? The parish system was meant to ensure that everyone had ministerial support - but can it mean that no one else can minister or set up a church? Preaching should open God's Word to everyone - but can it mean that people cannot find God for themselves through Scripture? The clothes we wear, the times of worship, the language, the seats we sit on and everything we do is subject to the same scrutiny by Jesus.

Ask someone new to your church - and with a different country of origin, perhaps - what they find in your worship that hinders rather than helps. Can this be changed?

---

[1] Ps 90:1 [2] John 10:18

DIVIDE AND CONQUER

'I will sing of your love and justice.'[1] Express your praise to God, using the words of hymns and songs that help you.

MARK 11:27–33

We are right back in the heart of things – walking with Jesus in the temple courts. By stopping the sacrificial procedures and in the dramatic action of cursing the fig tree, Jesus had indicated that the whole temple approach was doomed. With its wealthy priests, its meticulous but ultimately self-serving scribes, and its insistence on controlling access to God by ensuring regular sacrifice, the temple was now under God's judgement. The King had arrived to restore mercy and justice for all – including, it would seem, the Gentiles! The temple mountain itself, Mount Zion, was going to go though tumultuous experiences (*see* vs 22–24).

All this was not lost on the priests and scribes – neither the message nor the implications for them. Jesus' action was a direct challenge to their authority. It was important to trap Jesus, to trip him up and so to expose the incipient heresy that he was acting for God. Then removing him would become possible, in spite of his popularity with the crowds. Unfortunately for them, Jesus saw through their question and returned it with interest. The priests could not answer Jesus' question about John's authority as they wanted to because of Jesus' popularity with the crowd. In admitting 'We don't know', they were in effect saying that they were not properly equipped to handle issues of divine authorisation. They preferred their own comfort and popular approval before the divine truth. So do most of us, at least some of the time. More worrying is the recognition that in compromising we may have lost our ability to discern God's ways and the moral strength to obey. Both in personal decisions and in the varied relations between the Christian community and the political states in which we live, this cutting encounter offers us an example to follow.

Pray for yourself, that God will show up your compromises, and for leaders in your church, that they will put Christ first, whatever the cost.

[1] Ps 101:1

MURDER MOST FOUL

'I am the true vine ... Remain in me.'[1] Spend time enjoying your relationship with Jesus.

MARK 12:1–12

Many of our best hymns and songs relate to biblical stories, verses and passages, and we appreciate them much better when we understand this background. So sometimes we are given biblical references to aid exploration. It is the same here. We have an exciting parable with contemporary resonance and a climactic but tragic end. Yet to understand it fully, we need to know that Jesus is building on a song which Isaiah sang – we find it in Isaiah 5:1-7.

There are two vital aspects to note. First, although Isaiah's song is really addressed to those in Israel who have the responsibility of judging in Jerusalem and Judah (*see* Isaiah 5:3), Jesus speaks to his disciples. Secondly, whereas Isaiah says that God looked for justice and righteousness, Jesus' parable emphasises the extent of his search (the owner kept sending servants, and finally even sent his son). The owner of the vineyard's unmerited generosity is shown not only by the extraordinary care he took to prepare and protect his vineyard but also by the many opportunities he gave the tenants to pay him his due. Jesus makes his critique very pointed. For it is the tenants (Israel's leaders), not God's people as a whole, who are accountable. Jesus has focused the responsibility before God on the temple leaders, the priests and teachers of the Law.

As Christians, we are in an even more privileged but responsible position. Not only has God sent us his Son, we have seen and responded to his great salvation. We have received the full measure of his Holy Spirit. Whether as leaders or as responsible members of God's church, we are here challenged, in the deepest of love, to repent of all our sins and offer God our all!

Consider this question: 'What then will the owner of the vineyard do?' Use this response: 'Have mercy on me, O God!'[2]

---

[1] John 15:1,4 [2] Ps 51:1

'FACE' – THE FACTS

'I am the LORD your God.'[1] Living God, help us to focus on you now, to clarify our commitments throughout this day.

MARK 12:13–17

The priests and teachers of the Law were trapped by Jesus – caught between their real thoughts and the crowd's support for Jesus. They dare not antagonise them, so, they set their trap. The Pharisees (the holiness party, deeply opposed to contamination with all things Roman) and the Herodians (the politically astute party, allied with the Romans for the sake of the people) approach him together. Few people like paying taxes, least of all to a foreign power. Roman coinage was the major currency – although some Pharisees wouldn't touch it, it was so unclean! On the coin that they brought to Jesus was an image of Tiberius and words proclaiming that he was High Priest and son of the divine Augustus – enough to upset even a mild patriot, let alone an observant Jew. The question appealed to a human reluctance to pay taxes, but it was more about nationalism and the Jewish antagonism to being ruled by a foreign power. Most of all, it was about loyalty to Israel's God. He forbad images, had promised Israel that she would always be ruled by a king of David's line, and had forbidden idolatry – all three of these were involved in this coin.

Behind this challenge Jesus saw the real issue – hypocrisy (v 15). In colluding together the Pharisees and Herodians admitted that neither party was that interested in Caesar's rights: rather, they were trying to defend themselves against the claims of Jesus on their lives and their nation's destiny. Today we face many complex issues where state and church or personal freedoms and Christian responsibilities overlap: abortion, embryo research, sustainability and carbon emissions, trade agreements, the use of military force, and so on. We need to ensure that we don't use the 'too complex' argument as an excuse for denying Christ's lordship over all our lives.

Take one complex issue you face – personal or societal. Ask God to show you where self-interest might cloud your thinking and actions.

[1] Deut 5:6

CATCH ME OUT IF YOU CAN!

Father, teach me to ask you for the wisdom I lack; help me to know that you can provide.

MARK 12:18–27

As far as we can see, Jesus is still in 'the temple courts', where he was left by his opponents.[1] Mark then presents Jesus as being 'in session', rather like a king to whom all would bring their concerns for adjudication. Jesus, however, has set the context for this session – it is the critical time just before God's coming judgement (v 9). So, what happens when we die? Like Jesus, the Sadducees told stories to make a point. Seven brothers who follow Mosaic Law each take on the serious responsibility of marrying their dead brother's widow – to produce offspring.[2] This law was not primarily about protecting the widow, economically and socially vulnerable as she was (hence all the biblical injunctions to look after widows). Here, offspring were vital to preserve the lineage of the brother and the inheritance rights which went with it. The story is fanciful, but in theory not impossible.[3] The intent was not to find an answer to a tricky court case, but to trap Jesus into antagonising the Pharisees and so give them even more ammunition. In contrast to the Pharisees, the Sadducees believed resurrection was ridiculous.

Jesus' answer is revealing. He teaches us not to project onto the 'other world' all the assumptions of this one. Inheritance laws will have no further function in heaven – so neither will this law. Secondly, he answers them through their own accepted text – the Pentateuch. Jesus shows them that there is good ground for believing in life after death – God is the God of the living, including Abraham! We do well to check that neither we nor those who ridicule our faith are making unwarranted projections from earth to heaven. Equally we do well to seek to answer them from their own sources of authority – whether other faiths or scientism.

Check out your own expectations of God – common (and false) expectations include prosperity for the righteous and avoidance of tragedy.[4]

[1] Mark 11:15; 12:12 [2] Deut 25:5–10 [3] See John 4:18 [4] See Mark 8:31–33; 10:35–40

WISE – BUT STILL LACKING

'Now is the day of salvation.'[1] Lord God, alert us to the special opportunities of this day.

MARK 12:28–34

I was eating in an Italian restaurant with a work colleague when he spotted a well-known TV presenter who would be just right for a project he was working on. He seized the moment, spoke to the presenter and gained his interest in the project. It was like this for the expert in the Law. He saw how well Jesus performed and thought he would test him: 'Of all the commandments, which is the most important?' How appropriate for a lawyer! He was no ordinary lawyer, though. Not only did he publicly commend Jesus – which took courage – but he added that loving God and neighbour was 'more important than all burnt offerings and sacrifices' (v 33). What courage did that take in the temple courts? No wonder Jesus said, 'You are not far from the kingdom of God.'

If we had the opportunity to ask Jesus anything, what would it be? Why did you have to die on a cross? Why is there so much suffering in the world? Why did my dearest have to die so painfully? (Or even more poignantly, why are they dying now?) What is life like after death? Whatever our question, as long as it was sincere, we would receive a courteous and incisive answer from Jesus. Then, how would we respond? 'Well said!' – even if it challenged us? 'You are right' – even if it wasn't what we hoped to hear?

Here is a twofold challenge. Would we, in our responses to Jesus, be as courageous and insightful? Would we accept the challenge to take the step beyond affirmation to commitment? Soon Jesus, because of his love for God and neighbour, would walk to the cross as the culmination of all sacrifices, the demonstration of total love. Will we go with him?

How do we respond when people question us or challenge our beliefs? Do we do it with the honesty and encouragement that Jesus shows here?

---

[1] 2 Cor 6:2

FINE CLOTHES; FOUL DEEDS

'Have mercy on me, O God, according to your unfailing love.'[1]

MARK 12:35–40

'Not all men are equal' – or at least this seems to be the implication of Jesus' teaching here. Having immediately before commended one teacher of the law, he now condemns them as a group. Hypocrisy did not appeal to Jesus, indeed it offended him greatly. He knew that pretence with others leads to self-deception and this is the most difficult barrier for God to dissolve.

As he surveyed the behaviour of this religious elite, in every aspect of their behaviour he saw the same deep corruption. In the marketplace they wanted to be admired and treated with respect. In their place of worship, they expected to be given preferential treatment and for everyone to take note of their presence and their holy behaviour. When it came to great public occasions – like a banquet – they assumed they would be on the top table, seated next to the hosts, and probably they hoped to be asked to pronounce the blessing on the meal. When it came to their personal devotions, they ensured that people could see them. Maybe most serious of all, when they were performing one of their prime duties, adjudicating legal disputes, they would 'devour widows' houses'. Both Law and prophets emphasised the serious obligation of those called to judge. They were there to protect the vulnerable and the oppressed against the power and avarice of the rich and prestigious.

In this brief word picture Jesus challenges us to the core about every aspect of our lives. What is it that truly motivates us in each sphere of our living, whether public or private, religious or social, leisure or work? In each area we are challenged to check whether we show love for God and love for neighbour, or whether any or all of them indicate only love for our selfish selves!

Pray that this penetrating scripture will break through any pretences or self-deceptions we have developed and expose us to the awesome searchlight of God.

1 Ps 51:1

DIVINE ECONOMICS

'Truly my soul finds rest in God ... he is my fortress, I shall never be shaken.'[1]

MARK 12:41–44

And so for another contrast! Whilst those with power and plenty are grabbing all they can, no matter what the damage to the poor and vulnerable, how is the defenceless, poverty-stricken widow behaving?

Recently I was deeply challenged by a story told to me by the director of a City Mission. A man came to them. He was known to come from a very poor, almost derelict, flat and to have few possessions. He came to them for help, but not for himself. People had moved into the flat opposite and he had discovered they had no money for their gas and electricity meters – so he gave them most of the little he had; then they had no food – he gave them all he could spare. Now he made the trek to the City Mission to gather more food for them – he had no resources left to meet their need himself so he now put himself out to ensure they got what help he could muster! I think Jesus would embrace this man.

The widow in today's story shows the same generosity and abandonment as this man. Having no resources to depend on and no additional supplies to fall back on, she lavishes her little on God. But in God's eyes her little is everything. She is prepared to risk everything for God; she does it unconditionally and without seeking approval from other people. So, if God requires mercy towards our fellow humans and not religious sacrifices, how does he see us and our worship in comparison with my destitute but generous man? Here's another contrast: how often have I been so moved by the desperate needs of fellow humans, whether in the aftermath of an earthquake or the most recent starvation in Africa, in the subway near the station or even in my church?

Reflect on these words: 'Truly I tell you, this poor widow has put more into the treasury than all the others.' How then should we act?

---

1 Ps 62:1,2

SURVIVING

'We have confidence to enter the Most Holy Place by the blood of Jesus.'[1] Give thanks!

MARK 13:1–13

'As Jesus was leaving the temple …' Are those words simply descriptive or are they also symbolic? Jesus is now 'shaking the dust from his feet'.[2] He has attempted by action and words and by direct encounter and indirect stories to awaken the temple, its ministers and its activities to the requirements of the coming kingdom of God. But nothing has changed! 'What magnificent buildings!' (v 1). Indeed the temple was magnificent. It had taken decades, the best of materials and the best craftsmanship to build, but the big question was, 'Has it been built to glorify God or to honour Herod?' The next question was, 'Has it been built out of the generosity and gratitude of the builder or the taxes of the poor?' and the third was, 'Does it enable ordinary people to worship and appreciate God?' When these questions were put, the temple failed the test. That is why Jesus knew it would not survive, in spite of the apparent permanence ('massive stones') and prestige ('magnificent buildings'). Jesus knew this, because only buildings built on the foundation of obedience to God's Word really last.[3]

Yet, to see this truth, to speak it and to live by it takes enormous courage and steadfast faith. Jesus would exemplify it over the next few days; his followers would soon do so too. That is why rather than answer the question 'when will these things happen?' (v 4), Jesus helps the disciples avoid deception and prepares them for the endurance of faith. Social upheaval and national calamities are inevitable – they are the manifestation of evil forces within the structures of human life, just as earthquakes result from the movement of tectonic plates. Similarly, religious persecution and family rejection will occur, because loyalty to God must take precedence over every other loyalty.

Think through issues and situations (eg communism and capitalism; apartheid and Zimbabwe), seeking to understand them in the light of Jesus' words.

[1] Heb 10:19 [2] *See* Matt 10:14 [3] *See* Matt 7:24–27

WATCHING THE GOAL

Thank you, Lord, for revealing some of your ultimate purposes. Stretch my understanding through your Word.

MARK 13:14–31

This reading is saturated with allusions to the Old Testament[1] and the Apocrypha, which can make it heavy going for many of us. 'Let the reader understand' (v 14) is all very well for those who are familiar with Daniel and 1 Maccabees! It is helpful to know that in 167 BC the Seleucid king Antiochus Epiphanes had attacked Jerusalem and set up a pagan statue (an 'abomination that causes desolation') in the temple, and that Daniel's words were further fulfilled when the Romans destroyed the temple in AD 70. It is this last event that Jesus is probably referring to in verses 14–23. Then 'in those days' (vs 24–27) looks to the horizon of the second coming. It's possible that verse 26 refers to Jesus 'coming' not to earth but to the presence of the Father in glory (as Daniel 7:13,14 suggests).

The command to be on your guard, which first appeared in verse 9, is central to this section of Mark. The test of a true prophet is his track record.[2] When the temple was destroyed in AD 70 the accuracy of Jesus' predictions would lend credence to what he had to say about the last times.

Prophecy is often concerned with transforming people's attitudes. For the first disciples this meant understanding that despite the impending distress of the crucifixion and later the destruction of the temple, Jesus is always in control, and that his death, far from crushing their hopes, would lead to a far more glorious future, which would include disciples from the ends of the earth. We have missed Jesus' point if we allow apocalyptic prophecies to terrify us. Rather, we should take seriously what they have to say about the reality of evil and judgement to come, and live fearlessly with our eyes on the future.

Consider Jesus, who 'for the joy set before him endured the cross, scorning its shame, and sat down at the right hand of the throne of God.'[3]

[1] Dan 7:13,14; 9:25–27; Isa 13:10 [2] Deut 18:22 [3] Heb 12:2, NIV

STAY AWAKE!

Lord, keep me alert as I read and pray.

MARK 13:32–37

'Be on guard!' 'Be alert!' 'Watch!' This command, emphasised by the use of three different words in Greek, bridges the prophecies of the end times and the impending dangers of the coming night for Peter, James and John. Jesus will be supremely tested, and so will the disciples. While Jesus wrestled with temptation in Gethsemane, the disciples fell asleep - three times (14:32-42). Their failure to watch with Jesus was the precursor to their deserting him. For Peter, it led to his disastrous failure when he denied the Lord he so dearly loved (14:66-72). (Do Mark's words 'when the cock crows' in verse 35 intentionally forebode Jesus' warning to Peter?) Part of the disciples' problem was that they were oblivious to the danger all around.

Years later Peter could write, 'Be alert and of sober mind. Your enemy the devil prowls around like a roaring lion looking for someone to devour. Resist him, standing firm in the faith'.[1] He had learnt his lesson, and passed it on to us all.

Jesus' teaching about his second coming was not theoretical but practical. Instead of trying to unravel the timetable of the end times, we are to use his prophecy as a compass for our lives. He has left us with work to do: evangelism and teaching, serious prayer, works of mercy and love; and the Spirit has given us the gifts to carry them out. What are we doing with our time? Shopping, channel surfing, dreaming of our next holiday - or devoting ourselves to cultivating the fruit of the Spirit[2] and using his gifts?[3] Are we consumed with our own problems, or are we concerned about others? We should not deny our need for rest and relaxation, or a good laugh, but we may need to evaluate the balance in our lives.

Lord, please keep me alert and don't let the tempter sidetrack me from your purposes for me, as I seek to make watchfulness a way of life.

[1] 1 Pet 5:8,9 [2] Gal 5:22 [3] Rom 12:6–8

RECKLESS EXTRAVAGANCE

'Take my life and let it be / consecrated, Lord, to thee; / take my moments and my days, / let them flow in ceaseless praise.'[1]

MARK 14:1–11

Flanked by ominous forewarnings of what lay ahead we have here the story of one woman's devotion. From John 12:1-8 we can infer that the woman was Mary of Bethany, but her identity is not important to Mark, even though he reports Jesus' words that her deed will be remembered. Mark focuses on her action, and views it first through the eyes of the onlookers, then those of Jesus, inviting us as the readers to ask ourselves what we would have been thinking if we had witnessed Mary's extravagance. To some, her action was inappropriate in the extreme. The ointment was worth perhaps a workman's wages for an entire year. Just think what a charitable donation that would have been!

Jesus saw through the hypocrisy of the critics and into the woman's heart. Did she know what she was doing? I believe she did. Jesus had raised her brother from the dead. On that occasion[2] Mary had doubtless had her faith that Jesus was the Messiah, the resurrection and the life, greatly reinforced. She knows now that his time of suffering has come. She will not go to the tomb, carrying spices, too late, with the other women.[3]

The contrast between the woman's action and the expostulation of her critics invites reflection. Am I too calculating in my giving? Is there a place for reckless extravagance in the service of the Lord I love? Does my giving reflect my relationship with Jesus? Am I critical of others who give out of their love in a way that does not serve the church's stated priorities? There have been times in my life when I have known it would have been hypocritical to sing the words below. Think about them.

'Take my silver and my gold, / not a mite would I withhold ... / Take my love; my Lord, I pour / at thy feet its treasure store.'

---

1 Frances Ridley Havergal, 1836–79 **2** John 11:17–44 **3** Mark 16:1

BETRAYAL AND COMMITMENT

The readings become increasingly intimate as we approach the cross. Draw closer to your Saviour.

MARK 14:12–26

These readings are full of contrasts. In the previous one it was between the woman and Judas, between the abandon of faith and the calculating hypocrisy of self-interest. Here Judas' betrayal is set within the story of one who gave his very self for us. Jesus, who knew what was in the woman's heart, knew Judas also.[1]

We are so familiar with the Communion service in our churches that we may not realise the shock that the disciples must have felt when Jesus told them to eat his body and drink his blood – absolute taboos for the Jews. 'The life of a creature is in the blood.'[2] Of course, this is the point: 'without the shedding of blood there is no forgiveness.'[3] Many of our traditions place emphasis on the symbolism of the blood. We can miss the real encounter here, and celebrate only a ritual. The wine may be a symbol, but Jesus' shed blood is real, the atonement is real, our forgiveness and our fellowship are real. The life of Jesus courses through our own lives, individually and as a fellowship. Here is food for our hungry souls. Here are forgiveness, healing, wholeness, love and security.[4]

Every true disciple of Jesus Christ enters into this story as into no other in the Bible. Jesus himself made sure that all who believe in him down through the ages would be participants in the drama. We are all seated around that table. Yes, there are myriads of us, yet each of us is drawn into the same intimacy with Jesus and with one another as for those first eleven. We remember the death of Jesus in his living, empowering presence, a foretaste of the great banquet still to come. 'It is the future coming to meet us in the present.'[5]

Think about the implications of this – how our sharing in the blood of the covenant binds us together as a family of believers as it binds us to our Saviour.

---

[1] John 2:25; Ps 41:9 [2] Lev 17:11,12 [3] Heb 9:22 [4] John 6:47–58 [5] NT Wright, *Surprised by Hope*, SPCK, 2007, p274

BEWARE!

'Let us not make the Christian path any wider than Christ intended it to be.' So wrote John Bradford,[1] Protestant reformer, burned at the stake accused of heresy.

MARK 14:27–31

The darkness of the night sets the scene for the testing of all involved. Jesus proceeds in the light of his understanding of Old Testament prophecy, while the disciples act on the basis of a flawed self-knowledge. The contrast between Jesus and the disciples widens as the night deepens.

From Zechariah's puzzling prophecy,[2] Jesus knows that when he is crucified the disciples will scatter, be tested and refined. With his eyes fixed on the goal,[3] he assures them that he will be raised from the dead and see them again. The disciples, on the other hand, are totally occupied by the present moment. It is indeed ominous and confusing. They had had to celebrate the Passover secretly, Jesus had referred to his burial, and Judas had left them under a sinister warning. It was late and dark, and they were tired. Jesus tries to get their attention ('Truly I tell you', v 30) and prime them for what is about to happen. They cannot hear it. Jesus' words about going before them into Galilee (v 28) go right over their heads. They take in what he says about being scattered, but can't for a moment believe themselves capable of such desertion.

It is hard to hear truths like this about ourselves. When we hear them from Jesus, through the Scriptures, through the voice of the Spirit, through trusted friends, let's pay attention. Sometimes our reaction is 'everybody else might, but not me'. The choice is between preserving a flattering but flawed view of ourselves and heeding a warning that will protect us in times of temptation. John Bradford, who has been described as one of the holiest men since the apostles, was imprisoned in the Tower of London for heresy. One day, observing some criminals being led out for execution, he commented, 'There, but for the grace of God, goes John Bradford.'

'Lead us not into temptation, but deliver us from the evil one.'[4]

[1] 1510–55   [2] Zech 13:7–9   [3] Isa 53:11; Luke 9:51   [4] Matt 6:13

JESUS AND THE FATHER

Tread carefully. Spend some time in silence. Don't rush. This is holy ground.

MARK 14:32–42

If the disciples were tested in this story, Jesus' testing was supreme. Was there ever temptation like this? Knowing what lies ahead, he prepares for it in prostration before his Father and pours out his heart. Anything, anything, he pleads, but this.

These verses give us the privilege of seeing into the heart of Jesus at the time of his supreme crisis. Was there ever such emotion, such intimacy, such grief? Mark uses two unusual words here. The first, 'deeply distressed', implies terror. In the New Testament it is found only in Mark. It means to be in an intense emotional state because of something causing great alarm. The second word, 'troubled', means to be in anguish. The NRSV translates it 'agitated'. We see here a very human Jesus overwhelmed by intense emotion, agonising over what he has to go through. In the words of the Authorised Version, made memorable by Handel's *Messiah*, 'Behold and see if there be any sorrow like unto his sorrow'.[1] The man of sorrows was about to be wounded for us all.[2] The moment and the grief were cosmic.

How did Mark know all this, when the only witnesses had fallen asleep? Jesus had taken them to be with him in his darkest hour, perhaps for some human comfort, but more importantly that they might be privy to his struggle, and from it learn how to face the testing that lay ahead for them. I can only think that Mark learned about it from Peter himself, and that as part of Peter's later restoration[3] Jesus had shared with him the realities of temptation. Perhaps that conversation included some intimate sharing about cosmic engagement in prayer. It is here for our benefit. We share in Jesus' darkest hour. We come away strengthened to face our own times of testing.

'My song is love unknown, / My Saviour's love to me; / Love to the loveless shown, / That they might lovely be … This is my Friend, my Friend indeed, / Who at my need his life did spend.'[4]

---

[1] Lam 1:12   [2] Isa 52:13 – 53:12   [3] John 21:15–19   [4] Samuel Crossman, 1623–83

WHO IS ON TRIAL HERE?

Come to one 'who has been tempted in every way, just as we are – yet he did not sin'.[1]

MARK 14:43–65

Betrayal, violence, desertion, conspiracy, cruelty, false witness, unjust conviction. We have an ugly array of sins in this reading. Jesus' poise and his words in verse 62 soar above it all.

This passage presents us with some conundrums. First, the action of Judas, whose motives we can only guess. Judas, whose name is synonymous with 'traitor'. Mark brings out the depth of his treachery with the same phrase, 'one of the twelve', that he had used when Jesus predicted his betrayal (v 20). This was one whom Jesus had chosen to be with him and had even received the power to cast out demons.[2] Then there is the incident, found only in Mark, of the anonymous young man who makes a shadowy appearance, half dressed, and escapes naked (vs 51,52). Can this be Mark himself?

Then the kangaroo court, held illegally at night, hastily gathered in the house of the high priest, seeking evidence for a death sentence although only the Romans had authority to convict. Although the Sanhedrin had been in conflict with Jesus ever since his entry into Jerusalem, they couldn't find any charge to bring against him. Then they remembered Jesus' words about the destruction of the temple and twisted them into false evidence, linking them ironically to the veiled prophecy of his resurrection.[3] Even so, they could not find the three witnesses necessary to secure a conviction.[4] Jesus maintained his poise, infuriating the high priest. Finally, when asked point blank whether he was the Messiah, he quoted the prophecy from Daniel. Who is guilty of blasphemy now? Not Jesus, who is speaking the truth, but the high priest himself.

'Bearing shame and scoffing rude / In my place condemned he stood. / Sealed my pardon with his blood, / Hallelujah! What a Saviour!'[5]

---

1 Heb 4:15 **2** Mark 3:14,15 **3** John 2:19 **4** Deut 19:15 **5** Philip P Bliss, 1838–76, 'Man of Sorrows'

UNIMAGINABLE FAILURE

Lord, you know how hard it is to face up to failure. Help us deal with its consequences, and remind us of your covenant love.

MARK 14:66–72

Peter is alone, cold, tired, and afraid. At least he had not fled, like the other disciples. This is the Peter who was the first of the disciples to recognise who Jesus was. Jesus had called him 'the Rock', recognising his potential despite his weaknesses. Luke records how Satan had asked to have all the disciples to pick them apart, and how Jesus had prayed for 'Simon' that his faith might not fail. After his memorable encounter with the risen Christ in Galilee[1] and the outpouring of the Spirit at Pentecost,[2] he is transformed, with a courage that amazed the Sanhedrin, who recognised that he had 'been with Jesus'.[3] We may be thankful that this episode in Peter's life is recorded for us. Through his tears he may have thought that everything was over. (Consider his suggestion that they go back to fishing.)[4] Jesus saw otherwise, knew that his failure was a lapse, restored him and equipped him to be the great leader he became.

We are all prone to failure, even after receiving the Spirit, and perhaps particularly when confronted with a challenge to our faith in Jesus. Do we take these situations with the kind of repentance shown by Peter? Or do we make excuses to ourselves about being tired, or caught off guard? (What was that about keeping alert?)

Perhaps you have failed (or will fail) in other catastrophic ways. You may think that Jesus will never talk to you again, but don't despair. Take heart. Like David, who gave the world Psalm 51 after his fiasco with Bathsheba, Peter later strengthened his brethren out of his bitter failure: 'Do not fear their threats; do not be frightened … Always be prepared to give an answer to everyone who asks you to give the reason for the hope that you have.'[5]

Lord, thank you for your forgiveness, restoration and strength when I have failed; help me to be prepared for times of testing.

---

[1] John 21:15–19   [2] Acts 2   [3] Acts 4:13   [4] John 21:3   [5] 1 Pet 3:14,15

KING OF THE JEWS

'It was the LORD's will to crush him and cause him to suffer.'[1] Meditate on this extraordinary statement.

MARK 15:1–20

The Sanhedrin had struggled to find a charge on which to accuse the man they had already arrested, finally settling on blasphemy. They then handed him over to Pilate, who alone had the authority to pronounce the death sentence. They knew that he had no interest in the religious squabbles of his subjects, so a new charge was needed, one with political overtones that would resonate with Pilate. The crowds had hailed Jesus as king just a week earlier.[2] Here was a way the priests could frame him.

Pilate was in Jerusalem to ensure that there was no uprising among the Jews who had flocked in for the Passover. Presented with someone who was accused of trying to set himself up as King of the Jews, he sensed that something was awry. The man didn't look like someone with aspirations to royalty. Nor did he act like one. Invited to respond to the accusation, his reply was a model of ambiguity. What irony! The King of the universe stood before a provincial official who thought it was in his power to dispose of him. When a crowd materialised out of nowhere and clamoured for the release of Barabbas, Pilate took the easy path. Peace was restored. He had done his job. For Jesus, King of Kings and Prince of Peace,[3] the real, costly work of reconciliation lay ahead. He had renounced the easy way out when he had resolutely set out for Jerusalem.[4]

It happens to us all at one time or another to be accused of something we have not done. Jesus has left us with an example of how to handle ourselves. He didn't retaliate. He didn't lash out at his accusers. He didn't compromise the truth. Where did he find such poise? He entrusted himself to his Father, confident that justice would ultimately prevail. A challenging example for us to follow![5]

Pray for those who are suffering for their faith, that they will bear witness by their Christlike conduct.

[1] Isa 53:10 [2] Mark 11:10 [3] Isa 9:6 [4] Luke 9:51 [5] See 1 Pet 2:19–23

KING OF JEWS AND GENTILES

'Bow down before him ...'[1]

MARK 15:21–39

Mark's concise account of the crucifixion is written in such a way that the discerning reader will understand much more than what lies on the surface. You have probably noticed how the prophecies of Isaiah, especially chapter 53, underpin the whole story. Even more striking in this chapter are the allusions to Psalm 22. Jesus cried out the first verse of this psalm as he became sin for us,[2] obviously with the whole psalm in mind. David recognised that God is still the Holy One (Ps 22:3), prayed for deliverance (vs 20,21) and turned to praise, knowing that God had answered (vs 22-24). The crowd at the cross, conscious of the tradition that Elijah was the one who would deliver Israel, thought he was calling for Elijah and waited for miraculous intervention. Elijah didn't come. Mark leads the reader on to understand that God had a greater miracle in mind. The detail of the soldiers dividing Jesus' clothes is remarkable. Legal texts from the period reveal that Roman soldiers had the right to share out the possessions of the condemned. So, as well as fulfilling the prophecy of Psalm 22:18, the detail is precise in its historical accuracy.

Jesus' death is the beginning of a new era. Temple worship is no longer for Jews only. The significance of the torn curtain is underlined by the confession of the centurion in verse 39, the first instance in Mark of a Gentile recognising Jesus as the Son of God. 'Future generations will ... proclaim his righteousness, declaring to a people yet unborn: he has done it!'[3]

Don't leave God's presence without making this story personal. Confess your share in the sin that put Jesus on the cross, and come away with the joy of knowing that you are freed from its guilt and power.

As you thank the Lord for what he suffered for you, pray for the spread of this good news over all the earth.

---

[1] JSB Monsell, 1811–75, 'O worship the Lord'; cf Ps 22:27 [2] 2 Cor 5:21
[3] Ps 22:30,31

THE WOMEN DISCIPLES

Do you sometimes feel insignificant before God? As you pray, remember that if he cares for the sparrow, he cares for you much more.[1]

MARK 15:40–47

It comes as a surprise to hear of the many women who had followed Jesus. Mark had not mentioned them earlier. In keeping with the custom of the times, the women had remained in the background as they performed the practical services without which Jesus could not have carried out his ministry. Though not numbered among the twelve they were just as much disciples.

Part of the reason for their appearance here is that the preparation of a corpse for burial was a woman's role. We have already seen how a woman anointed Jesus at Bethany.[2] The role they now play is much more significant. While the twelve were nowhere in sight these women were present at the crucifixion, watching from a distance. They witnessed Jesus' death. Then they accompanied Joseph of Arimathea to the tomb and saw where Jesus was laid. They were the first to discover the empty tomb. After his resurrection, it was to women that Jesus first appeared. It was women who were charged with the responsibility of taking the news to the twelve.

It has been pointed out that if the resurrection narratives were a fabrication, the Gospel writers would not have made the first witnesses women. Jewish law was careful about the validity of testimony, and although it nowhere discredits that of women, in practice legal witness always seems to have been given by men.[3] But the credibility of the resurrection account depends on the testimony of women. As with the testimony of the centurion in verse 39, that of the women here inaugurates a kingdom in which there is 'neither … male nor female, for you are all one in Christ Jesus'.[4] Whether in the public eye or behind the scenes, your service to Jesus is valued. No one is unimportant.

Thank God for the courageous and faithful witness of these first women disciples, and think how you can serve Jesus today, whether publicly or behind the scenes.

[1] Matt 10:29,31   [2] Mark 14:3–9   [3] So they are not mentioned in 1 Cor 15:1–5
[4] Gal 3:28

A NEW CREATION

'Lo, Jesus meets us, risen from the tomb; / Lovingly he greets us.'[1] Rise to meet him today.

MARK 16

Can you imagine what went through the minds of these women when they found the tomb empty? Can you imagine their emotional state? Mark uses some interesting words to describe their reaction. The Greek says that they were stunned out of their minds (TNIV 'alarmed', v 5). Similarly in verse 8, they were gripped by *ekstasis*, literally, 'standing outside of oneself'. In other words, they were out of their senses, amazed, astonished, in a state of distraction, confusion, terror and perhaps even ecstasy. No wonder. He is risen. Nothing like this has happened before or since.

Ever since I came face to face with the risen Lord at the age of 16, I have known in my heart that he is alive. But to put my head around this fact has been a different matter. Until, that is, I came to see that we cannot think about the resurrection in the way we normally think about the world. This event breaks all our normal ways of thinking. Which, when you think about it, is just what you would expect.

To quote Tom Wright, the resurrection 'is the defining, central, prototypical event of the new creation, the world which is being born with Jesus. If we are even to glimpse this new world, let alone enter it, we will need a different kind of knowing, a knowing which involves us in new ways, a … whole-person engagement and involvement for which the best shorthand is "love".'[2] Do you believe? Do you love him? The story does not end here. The Lord still calls his faithful witnesses, men and women of every race, to work with him towards that day when the new heaven and earth are here in all their fullness and there will be no more death or mourning or crying or pain.[3] Our 'whole-person engagement and involvement' with him leads us into a new way of thinking and a wider reality than we ever dreamed of.

'Ransomed, healed, restored, forgiven, / Who like me his praise should sing?'[4]

---

[1] EL Budry, 1854–1932, 'Thine be the glory' [2] 'Can a scientist believe in the resurrection?', 2007 [3] Rev 21:1–4 [4] HF Lyte, 1793–1847, 'Praise, my soul'

FOR FURTHER STUDY

Here are some other resources from Scripture Union to help you keep on reading the Bible regularly – in your small group and individually:

Whitney Kuniholm, *Essential 100*, Scripture Union 2010 – a comprehensive overview of the Bible including introductions for different sections, 100 readings with notes, and opportunities to pray and respond. It encourages a holistic head and heart engagement with the Bible alongside intimacy with God.

John Grayston, *Explorer's Guide to the Bible*, Scripture Union, 2008 – for anyone who wants to know more about the Bible but isn't an expert. The book is divided into three main sections to give readers different levels of Bible engagement, ranging from a general overview to a a close-up look at each book.

The *God Moments Together* series: small group study material aimed at busy people who are juggling study, work, family, friends, church... These straightforward outlines will help you to meet with God as you get together with others to read the Bible and pray.

The *LifeBuilder* series: small group study material. Many titles including topical and character studies, Old and New Testament books.

THE WRITERS

Dr PAUL WOODBRIDGE is Director of Free Church Ministry Training and Tutor in New Testament at Oak Hill Theological College, North London. He is a football referee and a keen cricket fan.

GERARD KELLY is a founding director, with his wife Chrissie, of The Bless Network (blessnet.eu). He prays on twitter (twitter.com/twitturgies) and blogs on tumblr (gerardkelly.tumblr.com).

Dr KEITH WARRINGTON is Vice-Principal and Director of Doctoral Studies at Regent Theological College in West Malvern.

Rt Rev GRAHAM CRAY is Archbishops' Missioner and leader of the Fresh Expressions team. He is also Chair of the Soul Survivor Trust.

Rev Dr JENNIFER TURNER is serving God in several countries as well as her native Australia on short-term missions, training pastors and church leaders.

Dr ELAINE STORKEY is President of Tearfund, among many other roles. She has written many books, including *The Search for Intimacy* (Hodder & Stoughton, 1995).

STEVE BRADBURY was National Director of TEAR Australia for 25 years, and is now Chair of Micah Challenge, a global campaign against poverty.

Rev DAVID JACKMAN founded the Cornhill Training Centre in London, which he directed until 2005. He was then President of the Proclamation Trust until 2009, and is now a visiting lecturer at Oak Hill Theological College in London. He is the author of many books, including *Opening up the Bible* (SU, 2006).

ANNABEL ROBINSON is now retired. She was formerly Professor of Classics at the University of Regina in Canada. She is married to Reid, with children and grandchildren in Calgary and in Oslo, Norway.

Dr DAVID SMITH is Senior Research Fellow at International Christian College, Glasgow. He has written many books including *Mission After Christendom* (DLT) and *Moving Towards Emmaus* (SPCK).

Rev Dr JOHN HARRIS is Translation Consultant for the Bible Society in Australia. His major interest is in the faithful transmission of the Scriptures in Aboriginal and Pacific languages.

Rev Dr ALASTAIR CAMPBELL is a Baptist minister. Before his retirement he taught New Testament at Spurgeon's College, London and at the Union Theological College of the West Indies in Kingston, Jamaica.

Rev Dr STEVE MOTYER works at London School of Theology where he leads the Theology and Counselling degree programme, and teaches New Testament and Hermeneutics.

Rev Dr DAVID SPRIGGS is a Baptist minister, and is now serving with the Bible Society as Bible and Church Consultant.

Encounter through the Bible is a devotional Bible guide that can be used any time. It uses some of the best of the *Encounter with God* Bible series to guide the reader through whole Bible books in a systematic way.

Like *Encounter with God*, it is an ideal guide for the thinking Christian who wants to interpret and apply the whole Bible in a way that is relevant to the issues of today's world.

- Devotional Bible guide for use any time.
- Whole Bible books using a systematic approach.
- Helps you read through the whole Bible.

Look out for the other guides in the series:

Genesis, Exodus, Leviticus
Numbers, Deuteronomy, Joshua
Judges, Ruth, 1 & 2 Samuel
Luke, John

RRP: £5.99 per title

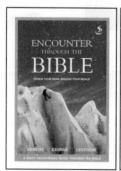
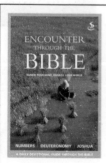
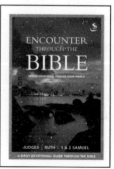

BIBLE READING GUIDES

Scripture Union publishes a comprehensive range of daily Bible guides, both in print and in electronic formats:

Encounter with God: A thoughtful, in-depth aproach to systematic Bible reading applied to contemporary living.

Daily Bread: For people who want to explore, understand and enjoy the Bible as they apply it to everyday life. (Also available in a large print version.)

Closer to God: For people who long to hear God's voice and experience his love and power.

WordLive: an innovative online Bible experience for groups and individuals.

Check it out at www.wordlive.org

SU publications are available from Christian bookshops, on the internet or via mail order:

* www.scriptureunion.org.uk/shop
* info@scriptureunion.org.uk
* 01908 856006
* SU Mail Order, PO Box 5148, Milton Keynes MLO, MK2 2YX, UK